THE GREAT CENTURIES OF PAINTING

COLLECTION PLANNED AND DIRECTED BY

ALBERT SKIRA

The colorplate on the title-page: Tavern Scene, Pompeii.

Translated by Stuart Gilbert.

PRINTED IN SWITZERLAND

THE GREAT CENTURIES OF PAINTING

ROMAN PAINTING

TEXT BY AMEDEO MAIURI

Curator of the Naples Museum

SKIRA

PRIESTESS AND GOAT. FROM POMPEII. MUSEO NAZIONALE, NAPLES.

ROMAN PAINTING

ANCIENT PAINTING IN ROME, POMPEII, HERCULANEUM, STABIAE, PAESTUM, CUMAE AND RUVO

VENUS ON HER SEASHELL. NEW EXCAVATIONS, REGION II, INS. 6, NO. 3, POMPEII.

ONE OF THE LATEST "FINDS," THIS SCENE OF VENUS EN ROUTE FOR CYTHERA HAS CURIOUS INTIMATIONS OF A MUCH LATER DEVELOPMENT OF ITALIAN ART.

INTRODUCTION

The fact that not one picture by any of the great masters of Greek painting has come down to us and all that beauty of which the ancient writers spoke with fervent admiration is lost beyond recall, lends a unique importance to the paintings made in Rome and in Campania during the First Century B.C. For, apart from their intrinsic merits as works of art, these paintings are all we have to tell us about the glorious, but sadly perishable, pictorial art of classical antiquity. Not restricted, like Etruscan painting, to tomb-decorations, they were closely associated with the daily life of the Campanians and figured on the walls of palaces, town and country houses. Few paintings have survived in Rome and Ostia; on the other hand, Pompeii, Herculaneum and Stabiae, the three cities which were buried under the ashes of Vesuvius in the catastrophic eruption of 79 A.D., contain a veritable treasury of ancient painting that enables us to follow the evolution of a whole art cycle, spanning nearly two centuries and brought to an abrupt conclusion in that disastrous year. Moreover, the study of this art period is indispensable for our understanding of the subsequent developments of art. For it was in this period that the last manifestations of Hellenism were petering out and a new spirit beginning to make its presence felt in the work of the craftsmen of Latium and Campania; that new approach to art which gave rise, in the hypogea and later in the catacombs, to the major trends (not so much conflicting as concurrent) of pagan and of Christian painting. True, this book is chiefly concerned with the great art movement which ran its course so brilliantly in Campania. But it would have been a mistake to try to isolate Pompeian art from its native background, that of the pre-Roman painting of South Italy, or to exclude contemporary developments of painting in Rome, which followed the same evolution as in Campania.

When first brought to light, Pompeian painting aroused vast enthusiasm. Then came a long period during which interest centered chiefly on an exegesis of the myths depicted; so much so that one has an impression that the specialists in question quite forgot that the objects of their study were primarily works of art. In other words, antiquarianism replaced appreciation. Today we can smile at these misdirected efforts, the controversies and hypotheses that often developed around a single picture without the least regard to its artistic merits. We must also remember that many of these pictures, both representational and decorative, were detached from the walls on which they had originally figured, with the result that both the compositional unity between individual paintings and the over-all decorative plan were lost, and, by the same token, the interrelations between the pictures themselves. Thus the orchestration, so to speak, of line and color on the four walls of a room was replaced by the presentation of isolated fragments, and in some cases of mere details. It was only during the last few decades that attention was diverted to the very real artistic value of these works and they were assigned their place in the lineage of ancient art. Yet, even so, they were usually evaluated from a viewpoint which did them less than justice. The method followed was that which had been employed in many other fields of art, that of positing lost prototypes and trying mentally to reconstruct these on the strength of what were taken to be more or less faithful copies. But it was too often forgotten that, though works in bronze and marble by the great Greek sculptors have come down to us, and we can trace the successive phases of that branch of art, all we have to go on as regards the paintings of Polygnotus, Zeuxis, Parrhasius and Apelles are the glowing descriptions of their work given by ancient writers. And much the same applies to the work of the later Hellenistic masters; they are little more than names to us. We are assured that they were great artists, but only the scantiest information is forthcoming about their methods, style and even the subjects of their pictures. In fact we have to content ourselves with the technical and aesthetic appraisals of their art quoted by Pliny who, though in point of fact he seems to have been more interested in natural history than in aesthetics, spared no pains in collecting all the data available, compiled a sort of *catalogue raisonné* of ancient art and included it in Chapters 34 and 35 of his *Naturalis Historia*.

What Pliny has to say about the artists themselves is lamentably meager. Thus he briefly tells us that a certain Fabius Pictor, first of the family to bear that name, decorated the walls of the temple of Salus in Rome. All we are told of an artist named Turpilius (an *eques*) is that he painted with his left hand; and of Titedius Labeo that the childish character of his art much amused the public of his day. Happily we have some-what better information about the painters of the age of Augustus and the early Empire. Thus we learn that Arellius used his mistresses as models for the faces of the goddesses he painted. This scrap of information is not as trivial as it seems, for it shows that Roman painters were reacting against the classicizing tendencies of the many neo-Attic painters then in Rome. Thus Arellius humanized his sacred figures, giving them the faces of real people, as was later to be done by the painter of Dionysus in the Villa of the Mysteries, and the painter of the *Venus and Mars*. The name of Ludius (or Studius) is better known. Both Vitruvius and Pliny are practically at one in claiming for this painter of the Augustan age the distinction of having been the first to include land-scapes and town or garden scenes in his decorative compositions. It might, perhaps, have been truer to say that he gave a new prominence to such themes, or handled them in a new way. The only case in which we can definitely assign a major work to a specific artist is that of Fabullus, a painter who flourished under Nero; his famous decorations in the Domus Aurea are known to us by drawings and watercolor copies of the composition and some panels of the " golden ceiling " containing figures. We are justified in seeing in this noble and austere artist a precursor of those great Italian masters who adorned the walls of palaces and churches with glorious frescos. We are told that, wearing his toga, he worked without a moment's respite on the decorations of the huge rooms of the " Golden House," and was indeed so much wrapped up in his work that the imperial palace became, as it was said, his " self-allotted prison."

There is a very great difference between what we know of Greek painting and what we know of Roman painting. The former is all hearsay: we have little more than a string of names of famous artists, a sort of Roll of Honor, along with some meager biographical data (mere anecdotes for the most part) and lists of their chief works. Indeed, nothing has come down to us—not a single painting nor even an adequate aesthetic appraisal—to sponsor the vast renown they once enjoyed. As for Roman painting, the opposite holds true. Few of the painters' names are known, and none is famous, nor is there any artist to whom we can attribute an *œuvre* of any great extent. On the other hand a very large number of their paintings have survived, mostly in the three Campanian towns: Pompeii, Herculaneum and Stabiae. Amongst these, the mural paintings discovered in Pompeii have pride of place, owing to the very thorough excavations that have been proceeding there over a long period.

The only signatures of Greek artists that we find in Rome and Campania are those of neo-Attic masters. They drew inspiration from the scenes and motifs of the late Hellenistic manner, or else adapted the themes of the great classical artists to small pictures painted on marble in the delicate encaustic technique. Dioskourides of Samos was the maker of those two exquisite mosaics, masterpieces of genre: *The Street Musicians* and *The Visit to the Sorceress*. The famous *Knuckle-bones Players*, a mono-chrome painting on marble and a perfect specimen of this elegantly sophisticated art, is signed " Alexander the Athenian." The name of an Asiatic Greek, Seleukos, is inscribed on one of the walls of the Farnesina House on the Palatine Hill in Rome, alongside one of the most mannered Roman classicizing paintings. This, being a mural, was obviously painted on the spot, but the Dioskourides mosaics and the monochrome by Alexander are works whose highly finished execution and small dimensions suggest that they may well have been imported (by way of the markets of Naples or Taranto) from the Greek mainland or archipelago, and were not the work of immigrant Greek artists.

In all Campanian mural painting only one work is signed with a Latin name, a picture illustrating the tale of Pyramus and Thisbe. It figures in the palatial home of Loreius Tiburtinus and is inscribed *Lucius pinxit*. Nothing more is known about this artist, whose name suggests that he was a man of humble origin. The same holds good for the mosaics; the name of only one Latin artist is known to us: " Felix," the maker of the mosaic on the threshold of the House of Siricus. None of the large-scale pictures in the Pompeian town and country houses bears the artist's name; nor is there any signature to that wonderful mosaic from the House of the Faun which may be regarded as the earliest example extant of the mosaic art of classical antiquity.

Thus it must be admitted that, in the field of Campanian painting, the modern art-critic, whose chief aim is usually to isolate and to define each artist's personality, has a hard row to hoe. For he has not the least information to go on about the man himself, nor can he learn anything about the activities of the various guilds of painters and craftsmen which undoubtedly flourished at Pompeii, Herculaneum and Stabiae. It is hardly less difficult for him to draw any general conclusions, in view of the great number of mural paintings he has to cope with, the wide diversity of influences and styles they exhibit, and the kaleidoscopic variations of artistic taste, due to the political, social, cultural and even geophysical changes which conditioned the development of Campanian art. In short, this vast array of paintings, all anonymous, sets exacting problems for the art-critic and historian. He has to distinguish between the work of genuinely poetic inspiration and the work composed in a topical vernacular, between the creations of the true artist and the repetitive production of the mere artisan, between the spontaneous self-expression (within the limits of his technical and artistic competence) of the Campanian painter and an art which is no more than a pale and passive reflection of neo-classical tradition. It must be owned that in this exacting task of sorting out and identifying the personalities of the great Campanian masters, by a close study of their composition, their drawing and their color, little headway has so far been made. Indeed it may be said that, despite the extravagant enthusiasm and quite unjustified disdain of which it has been alternately the target, this vast artistic heritage has not yet received the well-considered critical appraisal it surely merits.

There is no denying that a great many Roman and Campanian paintings, especially those of the Augustan age and those of clearly Hellenistic inspiration, were the work of Greek artists belonging to the last phase of various neo-Attic schools. Even though the painters' names are unknown, the fact that inscriptions written in Greek are appended to the figures proves that the makers of these pictures were Greeks, not Romans or hellenized Campanians. Thus it is clear that a number of Greek painters had settled in Latium and Campania, and were employed by men of wealth and members of the aristocracy for the decoration of their homes. But gradually, under the Claudian and Flavian régimes, the tide turned in favor of the native artists. True, they had been shaped in the school of Hellenistic and neo-classic art; nevertheless their work had a raciness, an immediate appeal that was something new in art.

A striking illustration of the way artistic taste evolved during this period (it is absurd to regard it as a period of " decadence ") is provided by the various sets of pictures of the Iliad and the post-Homeric epic cycle that have been discovered in Pompeii. That magnificent residence known as the House of the Cryptoporticus is decorated with scenes from the Iliad, a sequence of panel pictures whose style and composition display the art of the Augustan age at its best, and they are accompanied by explanatory inscriptions in Greek. In the House of Loreius Tibertinus there is a similar picture sequence, but here the captions are in Latin. And, finally, the paintings of the Siege and Fall of Troy in the House of Quintus Poppaeus, a man of letters who flourished under Nero, draw their inspiration far more from the Roman versions of the legend and notably from Virgil's Aeneid than from any poem of the post-Homeric cycle. In this connection we may note another interesting point; though Quintus Poppaeus had an elaborate silver dinner service in the Hellenistic-Roman style, it was a Campanian painter he called in to make a portrait of Menander, and but for an inscription (in Latin) stating the name of the person portrayed, we should have difficulty in recognizing in him the famous inventor of the Greek New Comedy. (It must, however, be mentioned that the extant bas-reliefs and statues do not give us any very definite idea of the poet's appearance.)

In this kind of painting, in which classical reminiscences and Roman taste are intermingled, the artist is hardly to be distinguished from the mere craftsman; in fact even the most expert authorities in their attempts to trace these paintings back to more or less famous prototypes (on grounds which sometimes strike us as far-fetched) are at a loss to differentiate between them. No doubt themes and motifs derive from some classical, or more likely Hellenistic, original; but we must remember that once a certain iconography had become so to speak " standardized," stock figures and stock situations were bound to reappear—as was the case with the Madonna and the Saints in Christian art—and there is no real need to posit the existence of specific prototypes in order to explain the permanence of certain type-figures and compositional schemes.

Though it is almost impossible to identify the work of individual artists, schools and guilds of craftsmen in the vast, multifarious *ensemble* of Campanian mural painting, two major trends can be observed. One of these is classicizing, and while by academic standards these works are unexceptionable, they strike us today as frigid, hardly more than slavish imitations of Hellenistic and neo-classic prototypes. But at the same time a revolt was in progress against the art conventions of the past, and a new, bolder handling of line and color coming to the fore. The artists sponsoring this movement treated the incidents and protagonists of the ancient legends on human, realistic lines and depicted ceremonies, scenes of nature and figures of everyday life in terms of their personal observation and with scant regard to the canons of academic art.

Naturally enough, these conflicting tendencies found favor with very different cultural and social groups. Thus conventional, classicizing painting held its own in public buildings, and in the sumptuous town and country houses of the *nouveaux riches*, who aimed at demonstrating their good taste by aping that of their superiors in birth and breeding. On the other hand, the pictures figuring in middle-class and relatively humble homes were unashamedly Campanian in spirit; their execution might be sketchy, but anyhow it was lively and spontaneous, and they got their effects more by their colors than by their drawing. Moreover, apart from any social and cultural considerations, all Pompeian mural painting from the first century B.C. to the year 79 A.D.—from the First to the Fourth Style—shows the growing influence of the local craftsmen and painters' guilds, and in decoration, as in figure and landscape painting, they achieved a personal language of no small artistic merit. We must remember that sixteen years before the eruption of Vesuvius, Campania was devastated by an earthquake, and this necessitated extensive repairs to the damaged buildings. No doubt the artisans played a larger part than the local artists in these restorations, but all the same this first catastrophe may well have helped the Campanian painter to break with classical art, and Pompeian painting to become more frankly Campanian and Roman in character—in short to develop on the lines most congenial to it.

Little as we know about the personalities of the artists, their technical procedures are almost as much of a mystery, despite the thoroughness with which these have been studied of recent years. Vitruvius and Pliny have something to say about the manner in which the successive layers of plaster *(tectorium)* were applied to the walls, and about the pigments used. But we are still far from knowing the secrets of a technique which strikes us as verging on the miraculous when we see how well these paintings have stood up against the march of time—for over nineteen centuries. When the layer of ashes and lapilli was removed the colors were found to have lost nothing of their former brilliance; if subsequently they have somewhat faded, this is because of changes of temperature, too rapid drying, or infiltrations of humidity. As for the pictures that were left unprotected, they were damaged by sunlight, frost and damp. Thus, though we must regret that in the course of the early excavations so many pictures were removed from the walls on which they figured, there is the consolation that if this had not been done, many of them would have certainly been ruined by exposure to the elements.

From the time of the earliest excavations (at Herculaneum) onwards, art experts and historians have given much study to the technical procedures followed by the Campanian painters. During recent years various specialists have sought to solve the problem by chemical analysis of the painted surfaces, but it must be admitted that their conclusions (sometimes contradictory) are not wholly convincing, and much still remains to be done in this field. One of the most hotly debated issues was whether the three techniques—*al fresco*, encaustic and painting *in tempera*—were employed separately, or the three processes were combined in the same painting. It has generally been assumed that the Pompeian paintings should be described as frescos, the name commonly applied to all mural painting. But there are several facts which militate against the view that Pompeian mural painting was of this kind. The true fresco-painter needs a moist plaster on which to work, but sky-blue, green and several other colors mentioned by Pliny cannot be applied to a damp wall; then again, we very rarely find that the color has sunk in below the surface of the plaster. It is also clear that in the decorative and figure compositions the colors were superposed on the tinted surface of the wall. And, finally, such corrections as can be detected do not reach down to the underpainting of the picture or the decoration.

Quite recently a chemical analysis has been made of over a hundred fragments and it would seem that the Pompeian paintings were done in tempera, but tempera used in a special way, the chief binding material being an emulsion of hydrated and saponified lime. The extreme brilliance of the colors seems to be the result of some simple mechanical process, such as repeated rubbing with cloth or some tool devised for this purpose. The encaustic technique was used only for certain colors (e.g. vermilion), for walls exposed to the open air, and for paintings on wood, marble and ivory. The amazingly good state of preservation of the Pompeian paintings is seemingly due to several factors: the perfection of the technical processes employed for making the plaster, the final layers being composed of marble (or alabaster) dust; a scientific preparation of the pigments used both for the foundation and the colors placed above it; a carefully proportioned admixture of the fatty (saponified) ingredient which served to neutralize the causticity of the lime; and, lastly, the mirror-like smoothness due to repeated polishing.

The painting in the House of Livia on the Palatine is an exception; here the tempera process of applying the colors only when the underpainting was quite dry was not employed. When recently some of these paintings were removed from the wall with a view to their restoration, it was found that they had been painted piecemeal, the joins in the plaster being apparent, as is the case with fresco paintings. This suggests that two quite different techniques were simultaneously in vogue; but further research in the great centers of ancient mural painting will be needed to clear the matter up.

Thanks to the meticulous descriptions of them given by Vitruvius and Pliny, more is known about the pigments used, whether made on the spot or imported from remote Mediterranean cities. The former divides them into two classes, " natural " and " manufactured "; the latter, by their colors, into " florid " and " austere." Moreover we have found many samples of raw pigment in various houses at Pompeii and Herculaneum which were still under repair after the earthquake of 62 or 63 A.D.

Here we are worlds away from the four basic colors (white, yellow, red and black) which alone, according to Pliny—though he is not as clear as he might be on the point—, were used by the great masters of Greek painting. In any case he laments the fact that the contemporary painters' elaborately composed palette was not productive of works of high artistic quality. Apparently polychromy and the use of juxtaposed, complementary colors came in during the 4th century B.C. and was carried still farther and perfected during the Hellenistic period. Amongst the Romans the taste for elegant luxurious mural decoration (prior to the vogue of revetments in polychrome marble) involved the use of pigments so costly that they were paid for, not by the artists, but by those who gave them their commissions. The following pigments, Pliny and Vitruvius tell us, were held in high esteem: minium and cinnabar which, mixed with colors of inferior quality—*rubrica* (ruddle), ochre and *sinopis*—, provided the various tints of " Pompeian red "; *caeruleum* (sky-blue) of two exotic types, *armenium* and *indicum*; purple *(purpurissum)*; green extracted from the costly copper silicate named *chrysocolla*; yellow *(auripigmentum)*; black *(atramentum)* of two varieties, *tryginum* and *elephantinum* (ivory-black); white made from several varieties of chalk, *paroetonium*, *selinusia*, and *melinum* (found in the island of Melos). We can still appraise the quality of the plaster and pigments used by the various artists—and indeed their technical proficiency or otherwise—by noting the changes that came over certain colors before or during the entombment of the three cities, and those that have taken place since the excavations.

According to Vitruvius six coats, three of sand mortar and three of fine-grained plaster, were needed to prepare a wall for painting. The surface to be covered was then marked out into vertical panels and horizontal bands, and the ground upon which the central pictures, decorations and ornamental details were to figure was tinted in the appropriate color. Pictures that were to be given a prominent position were painted on an easel, upon wooden panels smoothly coated with a layer of fine plaster; then the panels were fixed to the wall by nails or iron clamps. Unfortunately, few of these easel-pictures have survived, the plaster having crumbled owing to the rotting of the wood.

The purpose of this book is to give an over-all view, as complete as possible within its compass, of all the painting of ancient Italy (with the exception, for obvious reasons, of Etruscan art) from its beginnings up to 79 A.D., the year in which the great eruption of Vesuvius took place. We end at that date because it marked a definite break in the evolution of Campanian mural painting. Thus, too, we have been able to allot the space it so eminently merits to the " popular " painting of Pompeii. More clearly than any other form of Roman art this painting, which drew its inspiration from the secular and religious life of the day, illustrates certain tendencies which strongly influenced the course of pagan and Christian art, linking up the paintings of the Catacombs with the long tradition of Roman painting.

So vast is the enthusiasm that, largely owing to the interest shown in it not only by authorities on art but also by contemporary painters, Pompeian painting has aroused of recent years that it has often been hailed as nothing short of a " revelation," and is no longer regarded as a field reserved to specialists and antiquarians. Thus the present work, with its eighty-four colorplates, for the making of which the latest technical processes have been employed, meets a need felt by the modern art-lover and connoisseur alike, and on a scale never hitherto attempted. Here they will find, in their original colors, the most significant manifestations of ancient painting that have come down to us; works which, across the years, have lost nothing of their immediate appeal.

FUNERAL DANCE. FROM A TOMB AT RUVO. MUSEO NAZIONALE, NAPLES.

I

PRE-ROMAN PAINTING IN SOUTHERN ITALY

Just as it is in the Etruscan tombs that we find the ultimate origin of all funerary Roman painting, so it is the paintings in the tombs of Campania, Lucania and Apulia that tell us most about the beginnings of Campanian mural painting. And though this art took various forms according to the locality in which it was produced, the same artistic climate prevailed throughout the pre-Roman civilization of the group of South Italian cities known as Magna Graecia. This art owes less to classical Hellenism than to the bold imagination of the Italic peoples — Samnites, Lucanians and Apulians — whose native genius had been fanned to a flame by their contacts with the Greek colonists. To this happy conjunction of influences we owe not only the glorious work produced by the last Greek potters in Italy, with their typically southern fondness for ornamentation and lavish color, but also the few, but splendid, examples that have survived of large-scale pre-Roman painting. Ceramics and paintings are the two most characteristic forms of expression of this " Italiote " art, a creation of those Italic races which had been most deeply impregnated with the Greek spirit.

Such pre-Roman painting as survives in Campania and Magna Graecia is, like Etruscan painting, always of a funerary order; this is to say it, too, figures on the walls of hypogea, whose structure and dimensions lent themselves to representations

LUCANIAN WARRIORS. FROM A TOMB AT PAESTUM. MUSEO NAZIONALE, NAPLES.

of the exploits and titles to fame of the dead man. Likewise, the artists' technique was much the same as that employed in the larger tombs in the Etruscan cemeteries, a thin coat of plaster being applied to the slabs of tufa or sandstone of which the vault is usually composed. The same conventional tints—red, reddish brown and ochre—are used for the nude portions of male bodies, and white for the faces of women; whereas garments and accoutrements are treated in more vivid colors. Thus there is no denying the impact of Etruscan influence on the tomb paintings of Southern Italy, especially in the tombs of Campania, where, notably at Capuavetere, Nola and Abella, there was nothing short of an Etruscan overlordship, until the Samnites established their supremacy.

None the less, even more in evidence than Etruscan influence in pre-Roman painting is its remarkable fidelity to Greek art and tradition, tempered, however, by an ambition, no less obvious, to build up an original language of its own. Even the few works illustrated here suffice to indicate the gradual advance towards a free and personal manner of expression. Starting out from the painting in the Ruvo tomb (5th century B.C.) in which the stylization of the figures still follows the Greek tradition, we come by way of the Paestum *Warriors* to that lifelike and vivacious picture of a woman which figures in the tomb of Cumae (4th and 3rd century B.C.).

Indeed the whole atmosphere of these works is far removed from that of Etruscan art. As might be expected, the paintings in the tombs of the men usually represent martial exploits, and the artists have given especial care to the depiction of the glittering armor of the Samnite, Lucanian and Apulian warriors on their Field Days, while another favored theme is that of funeral games on the epic scale. In the women's tombs, on the other hand, we often have depictions of the women's quarters *(gynaecea)*. Visions of an underworld of gloom were, it seems, distasteful to the Italic races, and the scenes of farewell which their artists paint so often are pervaded with a feeling of serenity, an almost philosophic calm. And it was in the same spirit that they performed the honorific rites at the tombs of those who, following Greek precedent, had been promoted to the rank of heroes.

Though discoveries in this field have been relatively scanty, and though they cover only a brief period (from the end of the 5th to the 3rd century B.C.), pre-Roman funerary painting in Italy illustrates one of the most significant phases of Italic art; indeed a knowledge of it is indispensable for a proper evaluation of the superb mural painting which flourished at a later epoch in Campania.

THE RUVO FRIEZE

Ruvo (Rubi) was situated in the heart of hellenized Apulia, and in the necropolis of this ancient city there was discovered (in 1833) a fresco which is the finest extant example of Italiote funerary painting. In the same tomb were Attic red-figured vases of a period earlier than that of the local craftsmen. This enables us to fix its date approximately: the second half of the 5th century B.C. Here we are worlds away from any Etruscan influence, and in close contact with the spirit and forms of Greek funerary painting, whose transmission was facilitated by the nearness of Tarentum.

Over eighteen feet in length, this frieze is divided into six panels and runs all round the inner walls of the tomb. It is edged, top and bottom, by plain brown bands. The subject is a procession of women, moving from left to right and holding each other's hands, bodies and faces being uniformly shown in profile. Their attitudes and gestures are those of the classical Greek Chorus. Obviously we have here a depiction of the ritual " threnody " around the body of the dead man: a ceremony that also figures on the earliest funerary Dipylon vases of archaic Greece. This is not a scene of weeping mourners but a solemn procession of women who, moving to the rhythm of the Greek *choros*, circled round the corpse during the ceremony of the *prothesis* (" setting forth ") of the dead and who thus continued symbolically to circle round the dead man within the tomb. We have here a continuous procession of thirty-six figures, intercepted at three points: by a woman turned to the left (like the corypheus or leader of the Greek dance); by two youths wearing sandals and short tunics; and, lastly, by a man and woman, the former a cithara-player and the latter wearing a cloak. (The costumes and attitudes of the young men have a curious likeness to those of the young pages figuring in some Italian Renaissance pictures.)

The panel we reproduce shows eight of the women figuring in this endless chain of dancers. Here every detail—mantles uniformly drawn up over the head, locked hands, forward straining bodies, overlapping garments—contributes to suggest the swaying movement of an interminable dance, circling the tomb for ever; indeed the effect produced on the beholder is almost one of dizziness.

No less impressive is the counterpoint of vivid colors; the long, trailing chitons are diversified with broad horizontal or vertical stripes, and these motifs are repeated in the edges of the hoods, rendered in almost strident tones of red, black, yellow, white and blue. The harshness of the profiles is implemented by the sharply drawn chins and noses, the fixity of the women's gaze, the immobility of the big, circular earrings, contrasting with the surging undulations of the drapery by which alone, it would seem, the artist sought to convey the movement, solemn and violent at once, of the figures. For this dance in honor of the dead recalls not only the hieratic rhythms of a temple dance of maidens round the altar, but also the orgiastic rout of girls and women in the rite of Dionysus. Though little known, this Ruvo fresco is beyond question one of the most memorable contributions made by pre-Roman Italy to the art of painting.

THE PAESTUM TOMBS   In the funerary paintings at Paestum we find an atmosphere vastly different, both ethnically and artistically, from that at Ruvo. Here we are in the heart of Lucania, a district which, though it finally came under Greek domination, never abandoned its warlike traditions and funeral customs. The Lucanians, too, deposited in the tomb of the dead warrior his weapons and most treasured possessions, all in fact that might stand him in good stead in the netherworld. But they also placed in the tomb the dead man's likeness and a record of his great deeds and the honors done him at the funeral. The scenes were usually of a military order, with warriors and mounted men. In this connection it must not be forgotten that the Lucanians put up an heroic resistance

WOMAN CARRYING AN OFFERING. FROM A TOMB AT PAESTUM. MUSEO NAZIONALE, NAPLES.

when attacked by the Tarentine Greeks and held their own against the army of Alexander of Epirus, the most dashing cavalry commander of the period. They succeeded not only in conquering Posidonia (Paestum) but also in giving a typically Italic imprint to that famous city of temples—and in particular the greatly venerated sanctuary of Hera Argiva—on the estuary of the river Silarus.

In the so-called Tomb of the Warrior the " battle dress " worn by the figures is basically Italic, though somewhat modified by the influence of Greek funeral attire. This tomb may probably be assigned to the second half of the 4th century B.C., that is to say the period when Lucania was at the height of her military power and thrusting out towards the Greek coastal cities. The lay-out of this fresco is so disposed as to cover almost the entire surface of a wall, being 6 feet 10 inches in length by some 30 inches in height. Standing or on horseback, the figures tell out strongly against a neutral background, and the scene as a whole is enclosed between a red dado edged with the conventional spiral wave-pattern, and a cornice decorated with a meander pattern, above which runs a rosette frieze.

The two sides of the tomb are adorned with representations of Lucanian foot-soldiers and cavalry, who perhaps are to be imagined as parading in front of the dead body of one of their officers or a victorious general on his return from war. The riders show an easy mastery of their mounts, those mettlesome bay horses which were for a while the backbone of the Lucanian army. The footsoldiers who precede the cavalrymen have a finely martial bearing and march as if on parade. A standard-bearer leads the way, holding in one hand a lance and in the other a staff resting on his shoulder, to which is affixed a rectangle of cloth checkered with squares of vivid colors and a golden streamer. The accoutrement, in fact, bears out the description of the Italiote army given by Livy in his colorful account of the Samnite wars, and the contrast he draws between the drab, heavily equipped Roman soldiery and the enemy with their white tunics, flashing helmets and bucklers. The helmet worn by the standard-bearer is of the Greek type, protecting the cheeks and the back of the wearer's neck, but is adorned, like the leather helmets of the barbarians, with two plumes like the horns of oxen. The other warrior has a gilded helmet topped by a plume like a cockscomb; his cuirass is elaborately worked and the shield seems to have designs carved in relief.

A girl carrying a ritual offering, the libation goblet, is walking towards the warriors. We get a better view of a libation-bearer on a big, fairly well preserved slab from another tomb in the neighborhood of Paestum (at Albanella). Wearing a small black headdress, her hair unbound, this gracefully built young girl might have stepped forth from Keats' Grecian Urn. Wearing a long, sleeveless chiton of a deep reddish-brown hue, fastened by a clasp on the shoulders and at the waist by a yellow girdle, she carries a large drinking-vessel *(scyphus)* and an *oinochoe*, both of which illustrate the latest productions of the local Italiote ceramists.

The table laid with funerary offerings, painted on the small side-wall of the Tomb, is of an Hellenic type. Two ovoid jars, colored a rich lemon-yellow, figure on a shelf; obviously the painter wished to convey that these are not of common earthenware,

TABLE WITH OFFERINGS TO THE DEAD. FROM A TOMB AT PAESTUM. MUSEO NAZIONALE, NAPLES.

FUNERAL TOILET. FROM A TOMB AT CUMAE. MUSEO NAZIONALE, NAPLES.

but made of some precious metal. Between them stands a graceful *oinochoe* whose grey-blue surface, dappled with silvery gleams, also suggests an object of much value. On a lower shelf are a pomegranate and two big eggs drawn in outline only.

In some of the recently discovered tombs at Paestum we find the stock themes of funeral games, wrestlers and armed men engaged in single combat; in these last are highly effective, if rather gruesome, depictions of the wounds inflicted by spears or swords. While the decorations in these tombs have relatively little artistic merit, they illustrate the taste shared by the Italic races with the Etruscans for paying homage to the dead with scenes anticipating the gladiatorial contests of a later period.

Similar subjects (warriors in full armor, duelists, standard-bearers, horsemen, elegantly dressed matrons) figure in the Samnite tombs of Campania, at Capuavetere, Nola and Cumae; but the paintings in these tombs are, perhaps, of a more commonplace order and have less claim to rank as works of art. A notable exception is a painting in one of the Cumae tombs, which is far above the general run, and suggests what the art which was now developing in the ethnical group of the Oscan races in Campania might, under more favorable conditions, have achieved. It adorned the wall of what must have been a single-chamber tomb, as is evident from its dimensions (5 feet 4 inches in height by 5 feet 5 inches in width). The background is in a neutral hue; there is a wide red socle with a black meander pattern above it; the decorative band on the top of the picture has disappeared, but there are indications that it consisted of a Medusa's head, surrounded by birds in flight.

A robust matron, depicted with uncompromising realism, wearing gold necklets, earrings and a serpentiform bangle, is ensconced in a solidly built chair. Her face is fleshy, her neck thick and her big bovine eyes have the set stare of someone consciously posing for the artist; in her right hand she holds a gilt looking-glass. Her white tunic, richly decorated with stripes and arabesques, is held in at the waist by a girdle and her red cape, edged with black is clasped at the neck with a gold buckle. On her sleek black hair she wears a conical red beret, trimmed with a dark, white-edged band. So hieratic is her posture that one might think she is wearing a sacerdotal vestment.

We have here a typical Osco-Samnite lady of the wealthy class. Her racial background is evident not only in the heaviness of her figure, but also in the showiness of her dress, with its elaborate arabesques and gaudy designs. We may picture her preening herself in her mirror, approving of her bridal costume—for it is quite likely that the dead lady, an initiate into the Dionysiac Mysteries that were as prevalent at Cumae as in Pompeii and other Campanian cities, had bedecked herself thus for the ritual wedding in the realm of Persephone. Thus this portrait may be assimilated to that of the Pompeian lady taking part in the celebration of the Mysteries.

Facing the matron of Cumae is a slim young girl who, like her, wears a long embroidered tunic and a stole. She is holding a *calathos*, a receptacle serving both as a work-basket and for the presentation of offerings; and in the other hand an alabaster perfume-jar. Ripe pomegranates are issuing from the *calathos*, the pomegranate being a fruit symbolical both of death and of rebirth in the life beyond the grave.

Better perhaps than any other this picture brings home to us the change that was coming over Cumae after the decline of Greek influence in that city.

THE BRIDAL TOILET. DETAIL FROM THE ALDOBRANDINI WEDDING. VATICAN LIBRARY, VATICAN CITY.

2

OFFICIAL PAINTING IN ROME

On the wall of the François Tomb in the Vulci necropolis we have a scene of armed men fighting, obviously descriptive of some battle that actually took place during the struggle for supremacy between Etruria and Rome. And on another wall of the same tomb is a full-length portrait of Vel Satie, a handsome young Etruscan aristocrat. We have here an early illustration of the leading motifs of the oldest paintings of the Roman Republic: the commemoration of historical events, and the glorification of some distinguished personage. Born of the period of storm and stress attending the formative years of the Roman state, this art never lost touch with contemporary events and was, indeed, closely associated with the lives and deeds of great men of the day. At once commemorative and narrative, it comprised from the very outset the leading characteristics of later Roman art as we find it in the bas-reliefs on triumphal arches and historiated columns.

Important in this connection is a painted fragment from a tomb on the Esquiline Hill, now in the Museo Capitolino, Rome, and generally dated to the transition period between the 3rd and 2nd century B.C. This painting seems intended to commemorate the dead man's feats of arms and, to facilitate their narration, is divided into four horizontal zones, a conventional arrangement later adopted on a large scale on the columns erected to celebrate great victories. The technique is still that of Etruscan and Italiote painting: a black contour-line defines the figures, while the color within is put on flat, with touches of shading here and there to suggest muscular structure. All the details of the accoutrement, Roman or Italic, are rendered with such minute precision that some have supposed—rightly, we think—that these scenes represent an incident in the Samnite wars. What is certain, in any case, is that we have here the depiction of things that actually took place: a victory, a city conquered, a treaty drawn up and justice meted out. This interest in concrete facts imbues the work with an expressive vigor that atones for any lack of true poetic inspiration. Thus it strikes a note as far removed from Etruscan tomb-painting (whose setting is a limbo midway between the real world and the kingdom of the dead) as from Italiote, Lucanian or Campanian painting when influenced by Greek heroic themes.

When at last Roman art emerged from the silence of the tombs, its aim was still to celebrate the exploits of conquerors, and to extol their valor. Valerius Messalla led the way by exhibiting in the Curia a picture of the victory over the Carthaginians in Sicily, while Hostilius Mancinus, the first Roman to enter Carthage, exhibited in the Forum a picture of the siege of that city. The story goes that he himself pointed out and explained the various incidents to the crowds flocking to see the picture.

But now the march of history abruptly diverted Roman painting from the course seemingly marked out for it by regional conditions. As the Roman fleets and armies

IO, ARGUS AND HERMES. HOUSE OF LIVIA, PALATINE HILL, ROME.

overran the Eastern Mediterranean and the great centers of Hellenism, the result at home was an influx not only of outstanding works of art, but of the artists themselves, and their coming brought about a thorough-going change in the indigenous art tradition. Soon there was hardly a portico or temple in Rome that could not boast a painting by a Greek master; and these imported works were treated with the same reverent care that we bestow on them today. Indeed some Roman edifices became nothing less than public museums, and, as might be expected, local taste was profoundly modified by the revelation of these masterpieces. Doomed, it seemed, to extinction in the politically and economically decadent centers of Greece, Asia Minor and Egypt, this art now found at Rome not only the richest market of the ancient world, but also possibilities of a new lease of the life henceforth denied it in its birthplace.

But before long the Greeks commissioned to decorate the luxurious homes of the Roman patricians and their country houses no longer had the field to themselves; Roman artists followed suit, and with happy results. For they soon developed creative personalities of their own and, at the instance of Nero and the Flavians, decorated the vast wall surfaces of the imperial villas with works of real merit.

When, referring to official painting at Rome in the first century A.D., we speak of the Hellenistic style and the Roman style, these terms should not be taken as mutually exclusive. The two styles constantly intermingle and complement each other.

In Rome itself we find no traces of the first phase of Campanian painting, usually known as the First Style and illustrated by several decorations at Pompeii and Herculaneum. The earliest example at Rome of the new style of wall-painting is a work painted under Hellenistic influence that was discovered in the House of the Gryphons on the Palatine Hill which was buried when the Flavian Palaces were built. This was an elegant residence constructed some time between the end of the 2nd and the beginning of the first century B.C. The large *cubiculum* and two other rooms provide the finest example we have of second-style painting still in its most purely decorative and architectonic phase. The decoration comprises an imitation of vividly colored marble revetment plaques, seen behind a single row of columns. There are no perspectives or inclined planes, nor are there any figures, except on a lunette in the room adjoining the *cubiculum*, where two winged gryphons in stucco face each other on either side of an acanthus, much as on an heraldic device.

The first great example we find at Rome of the mural decoration of the imperial period is in the House of Augustus, commonly called the House of Livia. Whereas the near-by Republican home known as the House of the Gryphons was submerged beneath the imposing mass of the *Domus Flavia*, the House of Livia had the good fortune to be spared by the neighboring buildings of the *Domus Tiberiana*. And though this was not a palace but the private residence of the Founder of the Empire, it would seem that the leading artists of the day were called in to decorate the house—and this despite the assurance Augustus' biographer gives us of the Emperor's simple, **HOUSE OF LIVIA** old-world tastes. Indeed, while the four rooms of the west wing that survive have little interest from an architectural standpoint, their pictorial decorations on the other hand give the full measure of a mature and elegant art. These paintings may be dated to the period when the Second Style was at its apogee. In the center room are deep perspective vistas with a mythological scene in the center and, above, a row of small pictures in the form of panels. In the side rooms is a decoration stretching behind a row of columns. The architectonic lay-out, though quite simple, is diversified here and there with ornamental elements and reverts now and then, in the center and in the frieze, to the landscape theme. Thus we have here the combination of two motifs which, as we shall see, were greatly favored by the Pompeian painters: landscape views and scenes at once idyllic and iconographic.

Unfortunately this house is in a very poor state of preservation and it is difficult to form a clear idea of what these murals must have looked like in their original condition. Some, indeed, are completely ruined, while others, badly damaged, convey little more than a vague suggestion of their pristine colors. Most regrettable of all is the loss of the works in the center room, the *tablinum*, where the artist obviously excelled himself, both in purely decorative composition and in figure-painting. The architectural framework is the same as that employed, on a larger scale, in an alcove of the Villa of the Mysteries. The foreground consists of columns with acanthus patterns spiraling all the way up the shaft to the architrave; behind these are smaller, slenderer columns, supporting the epistyle of an intermediary cornice, while on the third plane are the prospect views of the central picture, and city scenes.

The left wall was destroyed in very early times, and the picture on the back wall, *Polyphemus swimming after Galatea*, has crumbled away almost entirely. The only surviving, though much damaged, painting is that on the right wall, illustrating the myth of Argus and Io. Jealous of the attentions paid to Io by Jupiter, Juno has entrusted her to the keeping of Argus; but, with his magic wand, Hermes (Mercury) casts a spell on the monster and sets the fair prisoner free. Such romantic tales of the loves of the gods were in high favor not only with the artists of Rome and Campania, but also with the local élite. Indeed, the upper classes had a predilection for those amorous adventures of maidens in distress which were the stock-in-trade of the Alexandrian *littérateurs*. As far as pictorial art is concerned, these themes originated with Nikias, a 4th-century Athenian painter. It is, of course, almost impossible to determine how much of the original conception of the Athenian artist has here survived. The composition, however, definitely recalls that of *Andromeda set free by Theseus*, a famous Pompeian painting also believed to derive from an original by Nikias.

FARNESINA
HOUSE IN ROME

Dating from the late Augustan age—or, more precisely, from the transitional period between the Second and Third Styles—, the Farnesina House contains, after the House of Livia, the largest *ensemble* of works figuring in a patrician home that has come down to us. Located on the right bank of the Tiber, it was brought to light in 1880 in the course of work carried out on a river-dam. A good many of the walls

GIRL DECANTING PERFUMES. FROM THE FARNESINA HOUSE, ROME. MUSEO NAZIONALE DELLE TERME, ROME.

and ceilings are now in the Museo Nazionale delle Terme, Rome. The owner's taste, at once refined and sensuous, was rather for intimate, amorous themes than for the monumental or impressive. An aristocrat with a fondness for Alexandrian poetry and erotic epigrams, he was fortunate enough to find in a neo-classical painter of the purest eclectic style an artist exactly after his own heart. This artist was, it would seem, Seleukos, for we find this name engraved beside one of the small paintings in the *cubicula*; it indicates that he was a Greek, hailing from one of the wealthiest towns in Syria. This would explain the rather studied preciosity of the decorative composition and the peculiarities of several of the figure-scenes. It would be tempting to identify this villa as the *Horti Clodiae* of Clodia, the beautiful, dissolute sister of the tribune M. Clodius Pulcher, generally believed to be the Lesbia immortalized by Catullus. But though the paintings themselves correspond so well with the temperament of the sophisticated, aristocratic Roman lady loved by the poet, there is, unfortunately, no doubt that they date from well after the days of Clodia.

In the House of Livia the wall space between the central panel and the small frieze paintings was occupied by architectural perspectives. Here, on the other hand, effects of depth are ruled out and, instead, we have a flat surface covered with a mass of ornamentation executed with amazing virtuosity and an obvious desire to make each detail in itself a thing of beauty.

The walls of a rectangular room, painted glossy black, are decorated with vine-leaf festoons, hung between columns, whose shafts are as dainty as acanthus stems, while the long frieze represents a series of judgments pronounced by King Bocchoris of Egypt, whose wisdom and understanding of human nature were as renowned as Solomon's—thus testifying to the interest of both the artist and the owner of the house in Graeco-Oriental themes.

THE ALDOBRANDINI WEDDING. VATICAN LIBRARY, VATICAN CITY.

The neo-classic mannerism of these paintings comes out most clearly on the walls of an alcove where, rendered with a minimum of brushstrokes, small figures tell out on a white background. Their elegance of attitude and expression recalls the scenes depicted with such exquisite lightness and charm on the milk-white surfaces of Greek *lekythoi*. A delightful example of this refined artistry is Aphrodite, seated on her throne in the attitude of a modest Persephone, while one of the Graces toys with her veil and a winged Eros stands beside them holding his scepter. The figure of a young girl decanting perfume is painted with such simplicity and elegance that we could easily believe it to be the handiwork of some famous Attic vase-painter. Yet actually we have here the work of a versatile neo-classical artist, whose erudite academicism makes itself felt most clearly in the paintings linking up with the center panel: banquet scenes and amorous encounters, also deriving from the Hellenistic models then in vogue.

If we except the so-called " grotesques " in the *Domus Aurea* and the wonderful decorations of the " golden ceiling," no Roman painting aroused so much enthusiasm as *The Aldobrandini Wedding*. The date of its discovery is not precisely fixed, but was probably round about 1605. It owes its name to the fact that its first owner was Cardinal Cintio Aldobrandini, to whose residence it was taken in the first instance. Doubtless its thorough-going eclecticism accounts for its immediate popularity; it was copied by many of the foreign and Italian painters who had been drawn to Rome by the fascination of the Roman monuments and works of art: amongst them Rubens, Van Dyck, Pietro da Cortona and Poussin. This admiration did not prevent its falling victim to restorers and retouchings, which, however, were subsequently effaced.

This frieze, now in the Vatican Library, seems to have formed part of the decoration of a small room, probably the retiring room, in a big mansion. Probably there was nothing more beneath it than an architectural pattern of festoons and caryatids, such as we see in the House of the Cryptoporticus at Pompeii; in any case it belongs to the late phase of the Second Style and to the age of Augustus. The preparations for a marriage are taking place in the privacy of a gynaeceum, and the scene is treated panoramically. Unornamented pillars indicate the division of this part of the house into *cubicula*, and the alcove containing the marriage couch occupies the center of the composition. On the left is the wardrobe or dressing-room, which often in Pompeian houses was no more than a cupboard-like recess. On the right is the *procoeton* (vestibule). In these three rooms, linked together by the architectural lay-out, ten figures are arranged in three groups, each engaged in specific, different, occupations. An idealized depiction of the traditional wedding ceremony, this scene has affinities, both as to its ambiance and its genre, with the Greek approach to such themes; for it is not purely realistic but, as in the ritual of the Mysteries, human and divine elements are intermingled.

In the center we see the bride, wearing her veil, lost in thought. Seated beside her on the end of the *thalamus*, Peitho (or Aphrodite) is gently caressing her, trying to reconcile her to accepting the change in her estate. Near by is a young woman, a Charis

31

(Grace) perhaps, pouring scented oil. On the other side is seated a sturdily built youth, his head garlanded with flowers and ivy. This is Hymenaeus, the tutelary god of marriage; he is watching for the outcome of the colloquy between the central figure, the timid bride, and the persuasive goddess.

On the extreme left is a woman whose head is draped in a mantle, perhaps the mother of the bride; she is dipping her hand in a bronze basin, as if to test the warmth of the water. In the vestibule three women are grouped round a *thymiaterion*: while one of them pours the aromatic incense, another, holding a lyre, is singing the epithalamium (nuptial hymn). The third, who wears a crown, is waiting to give final instructions for the performance of the marriage rite. The three scenes are linked together physically so to speak, and not merely symbolically, and the suggestion which has been made that this scene is quite unrealistic seems uncalled for. It represents the last phase of the marriage ceremony, after all the preliminary formalities have been carried out. While the women are making ready the ritual ablution and the perfumes, the bride sits pale and trembling with apprehension. Happily the kindly counsels of the goddess beside her will nerve her soon to face the ordeal and presently Hymenaeus will spring to his feet to summon the bridegroom, singing the nuptial song.

Neo-classical as are the composition and mood of this painting, it is charged with very real human emotion, and the artist was not merely working to a Greek convention. Indeed the troubled expression on the bride's face, recalling as it does the look of apprehension we find in the faces of some of the women in the Villa of the Mysteries, seems more in keeping with the spirit of Roman tradition than with the Greek view of life. Also, the detail of the woman testing the temperature of the water strikes a realistic note, typically Roman in its evidence of the artist's preoccupation with literal exactitude and incongruous with the Hellenistic treatment of similar scenes.

In short, while this wedding scene is for the most part idealized in the Hellenistic manner, it displays the same mingling of the Roman spirit and Alexandrian lyricism that we find in the famous *Epithalamium* composed by Catullus in honor of the wedding of Manlius Torquatus and Vinia Aurunculeia.

ODYSSEY LANDSCAPES

The art of landscape-painting is well represented in Rome. According to Pliny the " inventor " of the genre was a certain Ludius (or Studius), who flourished in the age of Augustus. We should be inclined to put it differently and say that to him is due the credit of introducing a greater variety of motifs and assigning a larger place to landscape in the field of mural decoration.

The painting on a monochrome ground (generally known as the " yellow frieze ") in the House of Livia on the Palatine Hill is a very fine specimen of Roman landscape art. Though drawing inspiration from the streets and countryside, it depicts some country far oversea: Graeco-Roman Egypt perhaps, or the coast of Asia Minor. Houses, trees, people and animals, all alike are bathed in the glow of a fiery sunset and can hardly be distinguished from the shadows they cast on the ground. What we have here is, in fact, a *tour de force* in the use of a single color.

It was a common practice to enliven the interiors of houses by bringing in pleasant and refreshing scenes of nature from the out-of-doors, and to create the illusion of those elaborately laid out gardens, a taste for which the Romans had inherited from the Hellenistic lands of the East. A striking example of this kind of decoration can be seen in the Roman Villa of Livia at Prima Porta, where the entire wall surface of a room, half sunken underground, has been magically transformed into the panorama of some garden of a dream.

However, original as these works may seem, landscape-painting had certainly a remoter origin. This is proved by the settings, rich in poetic overtones, used by certain artists for their depictions of incidents culled from the great epic poems. And pride of place must be given to the marvellous " Landscapes from the Odyssey " in the Vatican Library, Rome.

ULYSSES IN THE LAND OF THE LESTRYGONIANS. LANDSCAPE FROM THE ODYSSEY. VATICAN LIBRARY, VATICAN CITY.

They were discovered in 1848, during the excavations on the Esquiline Hill, in the arcade of a Roman house. The composition, which is 44½ feet long by 5 feet in height, comprises, following the procedure normal to the Second Style, the representation of a colonnade in the foreground, which is thus divided into eight compartments. But behind the painted architectural framework lies a continuous stretch of landscape. The theme is taken from that most romantic of poems, and richest in magic lore: the Odyssey; and painting and poetry are united in this great picture to the happiest effect. The subjects of the eight sections which are all that survive of the original can be easily identified; they are episodes from Books X and XI of the Odyssey. The painter has depicted Ulysses' encounter with the Lestrygonians, his stay on Circe's island, and his descent to the netherworld. He shows remarkable discernment in his selection of the elements which, for us today no less than in his time, lend its magical enchantment to the tale—glimpses of the strange lands and perilous shores visited by the waveworn wanderer on his long homeward voyage. For instead of assigning the leading role to the legendary heroes, the painter has subordinated the human element to the landscape and conjured up fantastic visions of the scenes of Ulysses' adventures, giving free rein to his creative imagination.

In these pictures the artist employs a plunging, not an horizontal, perspective, giving a bird's-eye view of the hills and valleys in which Ulysses and his companions went their precarious ways. Nothing could be more impressive than his vision of the grim abode of the Lestrygonians, with its caves and reefs and beetling cliffs, its twisted trees lashed by the seawind. Haughty-looking women and brigands from the hills are attacking Ulysses' ships and thrusting them back into a raging sea bathed in an eerie, almost Arctic sheen. On the other hand, in the scene of the first encounter between Circe and the hero, the sorceress's house suggests the glamorous palace of a fairy tale; while the artist's vision of the Homeric Hades has the rich fantasy of a Doré illustration to a scene of Dante's *Inferno*. In the cavern plunging into a cliff covered with queer marsh-plants and traversed by a livid shaft of light, whither Ulysses has come to ask counsel of the shade of Tiresias, we see the phantasms of the dead heroes massed around the pool of blood, and the artist's evocation of the atmosphere of the netherworld is a brilliant counterpart of Homer's unforgettable description of those regions.

As in the " yellow frieze " in the House of Livia, these scenes from the Odyssey are purely imaginary landscapes. Thus they have affinities with that " impressionist " treatment of landscape which we find in later works, with figures rapidly sketched in without any great regard to anatomical details. The air seems to shimmer in an iridescent mist hovering on land and sea, and subtle gradations of color contribute to an evocation of the landscape of a dream.

3

THE MURAL PAINTING OF CAMPANIA

At Rome most of the first-century paintings that have come down to us were in palaces and the emperors' country houses; thus, naturally enough, in all alike the stamp of patrician taste is unmistakable. In Campania, on the other hand, most of the pictures that have survived figured in ordinary dwelling-houses and only rarely in public buildings or the homes of the aristocracy. Pompeii, Herculaneum and Stabiae were the chief centers of Campanian art and all three towns were overwhelmed by the catastrophic eruption of Vesuvius which took place in the year 79 A.D. By a curious dispensation of fate the survival of so many paintings—an artistic heritage both fragile and intrinsically perishable—is due to the catastrophe itself and the manner in which the towns were buried by the ashes from the volcano.

In the pictorial decorations of these three art centers, fellow victims of a tragic doom, we find as it were a common language. This is because their historical and cultural evolution proceeded on much the same lines and a similar artistic climate fostered the development of both decorative and figure painting throughout Campania. None the less, though in all these towns the general lay-out and most favored themes (drawn from mythology and the heroic sagas of the past) were more or less identical, we can trace different artistic trends in the work produced, and influences of local masters and art schools can be detected in the choice of subjects, techniques and color schemes.

Excavations have been in progress at Pompeii for over two centuries; in fact they have continued, almost without a break, since 1748. Thus we have retrieved in the buried cities a very large number of mural paintings covering the period between the end of the 2nd century B.C. and the year 79 A.D. It is therefore possible to follow chronologically the changes in Pompeian art during the political upheavals and rebuildings of the city during those eventful years. Moreover the technical procedures of the artists, the nature of the pigments and the tools employed, can be learnt to some extent by a close study of the paintings which were left unfinished. The Pompeians had a great liking for mural decorations; they figured in the houses of people of all ranks of society, even in shops and workrooms. The subjects of these pictures were extraordinarily varied, and the ways in which they were treated differed according to the tastes and exigencies of the persons commissioning them. These decorations range from the *megalographia* in the Villa of the Mysteries to quite small paintings in *lararia*; from depictions of episodes in the Homeric epics to scenes of patrician life in the Forum; from glimpses of the women's daily life in the privacy of an Hellenistic gynaeceum to tavern brawls; from the savagery of the Centaurs in the palace of Pirithous to a sanguinary riot in the amphitheater.

It should, however, be mentioned, in passing, that copious as is our documentary material, and thoroughly as it has been investigated and collated by our experts, it has failed so far to yield all the information we had hoped for regarding the cultural, economic and social life of a Campanian city.

There was some justification for the procedure, followed in earlier times, of detaching paintings from the walls, but recently new methods have been devised, ensuring their preservation *in situ*. Thus the visitor to Pompeii has the advantage of seeing a number of houses with the lay-out of their decorations exactly as it was originally, and thanks to this we get a clear idea of what was the chief purpose of ancient painting: to decorate an entire wall, an entire room or even a whole house. Obviously this meant that art and craftsmanship marched hand in hand; indeed they were identical, and it would be a mistake to try to make distinctions between the artist and the craftsman of antiquity.

Being so close to Naples, Herculaneum was necessarily affected by the proximity of that essentially Greek town, bearing a Greek name " Neapolis," whose influence indeed is obvious in its plastic and pictorial art. Though relatively few paintings have been discovered in the portion of the town which has so far been excavated, they are all of great artistic value. Thus we have both the grandiose ensemble of the Basilica (in which the artist shows remarkable competence in handling the vast wall spaces provided by a building of this order) and also some exquisite monochrome paintings on marble in the pure neo-Attic style, which certainly originated from the Neapolitan marts and craftsmen's *ateliers*.

A good many of the paintings detached from buildings at Stabiae, which was excavated and stripped bare during the 18th century, are now in the Naples Museum. (It is only quite recently that excavations have brought to light enough material for us to form an idea of the admirable decorative ensembles adorning the walls of the country-houses built on the Varano hill.) Though its buildings are few and far between, the paintings at Stabiae display a variety of subjects and styles almost equaling that of Pompeii; thus we find mythological themes treated in the classicizing manner alongside almost impressionistic renderings of figures and landscapes; and no less striking is the boldness with which some of these purely Campanian artists rebelled against neo-classical conventions and followed their natural bent.

Thus a whole cycle of ancient painting lay entombed for many centuries in Campania under the ashes of Vesuvius, and while some scanty vestiges have survived in a few pagan tombs and in the catacombs of Naples, its most glorious manifestations have been almost miraculously preserved for us at Stabiae, at Herculaneum and at Pompeii.

DECORATIVE AND PERSPECTIVE COMPOSITION

All Pompeian painting was conditioned by its function of decorating the walls of rooms in dwelling-houses or public buildings. Thus its value derives from its acceptance of this function and can be appraised in terms of the artist's greater or less success in adjusting his work to the structure, the area, the character and the lighting of the place he was called on to decorate. We are so much used to the drab uniformity of the walls of the houses we live in that it is something of an effort to appreciate this function of ancient mural painting. But the truth is that the figurative compositions which have been detached from their natural setting—the surface of a wall—, or (a still worse case) such essentially decorative elements as Satyrs, Bacchantes, animals or ornamental friezes which have been isolated from their original context, share, if the comparison be permitted, in the unhappy lot of " displaced persons." True, this isolation of a figure or an ornamental motif may on occasion serve to focus our attention on its beauties, but it inevitably loses by its separation from the ambiance of the wall; and its formal, synthetic relations with the compositional lay-out of the room as a whole are nullified.

On entering any of the houses at Pompeii (and not necessarily one of the palatial residences of the wealthy class) we cannot fail to be struck by the excellence of the interior decoration, not only in its over-all composition, but in its use of color. Moreover, the visitor who has some notions of the arrangement of the rooms in the houses of classical antiquity can promptly see how skillfully the artists have rung the changes on various kinds of composition, themes and colors, not merely between one house and another, but between rooms in the same house. Thus there are alcoves in some of which an ivory-white ground is lightly decorated with candelabra-like stems of growing plants, while in others everyday subjects cover the walls; or, again, dining-rooms *(triclinia)* in which upon a vermilion ground the artist has painted landscapes, views or still lifes reminiscent of the good cheer served on the *mensa* (central dining-table); bedrooms with jet-black walls on which long white prospect views flicker into the distance like wayward sunbeams; or, again, walls the hue of gold painted with scenes of the gynaeceum to please the eye of some cultured lady. Nor must we forget the swimming-pools reflecting the blue of walls and ceilings, and real gardens ringed round by gardens painted on the walls, vistas of woven shadows and the flowers of some enchanted isle. Floors, too, were adorned with mosaic pavements, usually in discreet and tasteful black-and-white designs which served to counterbalance the sometimes rather exuberant colors of the walls. Unfortunately, hardly a trace remains of the vaulted or flat ceilings which were similarly decorated.

Everywhere, from the lordliest mansion to the humblest private home, the decorative scheme was based more on an adroit use of color than on the architectural structure of the room. Thus we have all the more cause to admire the skill with which these artists divided up the wall, vertically or horizontally, the just balance they achieved between the surface area and the composition, their apt choice of color schemes in which the colors varied according to their disposition on the wall (from the socle up to the frieze and the ceiling), and, finally, the creation of an ensemble at once decorative and containing figures. Whether the painter's field of action was a palace, a patrician country-house or a middle-class home, he solved the problems set him with the happiest results. Thus at Pompeii, where the houses were of very varied types, there was no less variety in the solutions thought up by the artists.

This is why in studying the mural painting at Pompeii we should refrain from fixing our attention exclusively on the intrinsic value of the various paintings taken individually and, rather, concentrate on the all-over decorative composition of the wall. It is customary to divide Pompeian painting into four styles, following the classification which the art-historian Mau drew up many years ago and which still is helpful. In point of fact, this classification merely differentiates the four manners in which the artists adjusted their decorations to the wall-surfaces at their disposal. But these four styles or manners did not only follow the changes due to the natural evolution of Pompeian architecture over a considerable period; they also reflect art trends which, stemming from Egypt, Greece or Asia Minor, were given a new direction in Campania by the creative genius of independent-minded local artists. Could a sort of anthology be compiled of the finest painted walls, it would be an easy matter tracing the development of mural painting at Pompeii and Herculaneum during the period beginning in the middle of the 2nd century B.C. and ending in 79 A.D. What, in effect, it would give us would be a graph, as it were, of the course followed by Campanian painting, which (not without halts and even occasional setbacks) advanced from purely decorative painting to spatial (i.e. three-dimensional) composition.

The oldest mural decoration was of an essentially plastic, structural nature (the "incrustation style"), and figures played no part in it. Obviously associated as it was with the house of the Samnite period, this type of decoration was certainly imported from the lands of the eastern Mediterranean, whence came the chief currents of Hellenistic architecture whose influence is so evident in the private and public buildings at Pompeii. But it was no longer sought merely to conceal the irregularities of the stone wall under a coat of plaster, as was done by the Greek architect when he overlaid a conglomerate of alluvial gravel with a uniform layer of very fine plaster of a marble-like smoothness. On the contrary, the Campanian artist diversified wall-surfaces with polychrome effects of rare varieties of marble, jutting cornices, and pilasters in relief, and made breaks between the different parts of a room. Thus the wall acquired a new importance, both plastically and chromatically, in the adornment of the house. But, in the absence of panels and painted views upon its surface, it gave the impression of being hermetically closed. To find a parallel for the display of imitation-marble in the Pompeian house, we have to conjure up a picture of the luxurious interiors that, after Alexander's death, prevailed in the palaces of the Graeco-Oriental dynasties: Attalids, Seleucidae and Ptolemies. The big naves of the Basilica at Pompeii, which were decorated in the First Style, have lost their colors; but a few small fragments that remain give us an inkling of the gorgeous effect produced by an interior whose walls had facings of this kind. The most striking example of this sort

FIRST-STYLE DECORATION. SAMNITE HOUSE, HERCULANEUM.

SECOND-STYLE DECORATION. VILLA OF THE MYSTERIES, POMPEII.

THIRD-STYLE DECORATION WITH MONOCHROME LANDSCAPE. FROM POMPEII. MUSEO NAZIONALE, NAPLES.

of decoration that has survived is in the first peristyle of the House of the Faun where in one corner the colors, though somewhat changed and faded, give us an idea of what the composition must have been. Here the decoration does not serve as a mere plastic and chromatic accompaniment to the architecture, but complements it, by conforming with the structural divisions of the wall. Thus *antae* balance pillars, while passages of black Numidian marble and polychrome moldings tally with the open spaces between the pillars. In fact, a perfect concurrence is established between the colonnade and the inner wall.

Another example of this, less pleasing to the eye, perhaps, but well preserved, may be seen in the so-called Samnite House at Herculaneum. The porch and the loggia round the atrium reveal a happily inspired adaptation of the methods of Hellenistic architecture to the traditional lay-out of an Italian house. The wall surface is interrupted by a rectangular recess of white stucco in which the door is inset and divided up into a high socle, a row of large slabs of imitation black Numidian marble, followed by a line of moldings painted in various colors—porphyry, green, *portasanta* and alabaster—ending in a cornice above which runs a frieze; and finally a second cornice of dentils in high relief. In the upper portion of this decoration we do not find an architectonic division balancing the elegant lay-out of the gallery of the atrium, but, surprisingly enough, two landscapes on a monochrome red ground. These are presumably the work of some later painter, whose manner foreshadows the landscape friezes of the Second Style.

After the adornment of the walls with plastic, polychrome revetments—i.e. purely decorative composition—came decoration creating the illusion of space by means of architectural perspectives, and it was on these lines that Pompeian painting of the Second Style achieved its subtle and elaborate effects. Motifs in relief gave place to a new kind of decoration; the wall surface was no longer limited to a single plane and the marvellous possibilities of color for expressing volume and architectural recession were skillfully exploited. Thus the extension of space *beyond* the wall, of illusionist depth, was suggested by the painter. And now we see the boldest feats of Hellenistic architecture figuring on the walls of the Pompeian houses. Approximating more closely to Asiatic Baroque than to any classical or neo-classical procedures, these scenes gave an effect of such compelling realism that Vitruvius declared himself outraged by them. Obsessed as he was with the canons of ancient art, he condemned much of this painting as being a sort of monstrous deviationism! Nevertheless what the Roman or Pompeian painter was then achieving was actually a great forward stride in the art of decoration. Though naturally he lacked any exact knowledge of the laws of perspective—the discoveries of the Renaissance lay far ahead—, he invented methods of rendering Space and of replacing the " blind," flat wall with luminous vistas stretching out into the far distance. These efforts to create an illusion of space are particularly noticeable in the smaller and darker rooms. But for the illusionist perspectives on the walls, such rooms would have seemed sadly cramped, like prison cells, since the only light that entered them came through the doorway.

Besides the great cycle of figure paintings illustrating the Dionysiac rite, the Villa of the Mysteries contains one of the finest examples of this style of painting. It is in a *cubiculum*, with two alcoves, that looks out on to the portico and " hanging garden " of the western apartment. On floor and walls, mosaics and paintings play their decorative part in this small but luxurious double bedroom. The lay-out of the mosaic defines the position of the *procoeton* and the alcoves, and the mural decoration, too, takes account of this division of the room space; thus while flat and plain in the main room, it includes prospect views on the walls of the alcoves.

Already in the last manifestations of the Second Style we find less rigor in the architectonic lay-out. A tendency develops to beautify the wall rather than to try to give it depth; and to employ painted columns, architraves and façades merely as ornamental adjuncts. Here we already have the characteristics of the Third Style, which aimed chiefly at ornamental effect. To it belong a large number of Pompeian paintings which, when discovered, were hailed as nothing short of a revelation. And their influence on the mural decoration of the end of the 18th and the early 19th century is plain to see. Once more the wall became " blind," self-contained; it came to life only

THIRD-STYLE DECORATIVE DETAIL. MUSEO NAZIONALE, NAPLES.

when touched by glancing rays of light. The wall space was divided up by columns slender as reeds, or by candelabra-shaped stems branching into flowered twigs. The panels are not decorative elements in any true sense, but more like pictures hung on the wall. Noteworthy is the extreme care given to details—we are reminded of the work of the illuminator—and this applies not only to the ornaments but to the figures, landscapes and animal scenes. Grounds of ebony-black glow darkly behind the vivid colors, emphasizing the delicate beauty of the friezes. Many of the motifs are of Egyptian inspiration and there can be no doubt that this style derived from Alexandrian Egypt. Yet the way in which the Pompeian artists handled it and the number of new themes they introduced says much for their taste and the fertility of their imagination.

The perfectly balanced harmony of the admirable mural depicting a monochrome green landscape on a vermilion ground reminds us of the elegant art of the Second Style. But there is also something new; that motif of the column, at once graceful and

THIRD-STYLE DECORATIVE DETAIL. FROM POMPEII. MUSEO NAZIONALE, NAPLES.

original, with its recall of the lotus, testifies to a new tendency, that of weaving forms of vegetable life into architectural features. The cold, metallic hues of the columns telling out against three other colors, green, crimson and vermilion red, create a strikingly original color harmony. This wall must have had its place in some elegant alcove; the delicacy of the style recalls the lovely bedrooms of the Farnesina House in Rome.

THIRD-STYLE WALL. HOUSE OF THE CEII, POMPEII.

In the House of Lucretius Fronto a wall of the *tablinum* (in a fine state of preservation) is in the purest " florid " style. Relatively small, it is divided into three parts, vertically and horizontally. A gleaming black background enhances the effect of the decoration, which has all the *finesse* of goldsmiths' work. The dado represents a garden scene; on the lower and upper cornices are scenes rendered in minute detail and ornaments delicate as lace embroidery; in the central section are figures and landscapes; while the frieze has elegant architectural motifs. The bright red-lake background of the central painting tells brilliantly out against the softer hues of the ornamental details and the figures, and the lustrous black of the wall. This painting comprises two scenes: the *Wedding of Venus and Mars* and the *Triumph of Bacchus*. Landscapes and seascapes on panels hung from gilt candelabra temper the rather fragile grace of the ensemble with accents of vivacious realism. The central portion of the frieze opens out upon what looks like the vestibule of a temple with a tripod in the middle, and doors on the sides. This arrangement became common in the paintings of architecture in the Third and Fourth Styles at Pompeii. Another very striking work is the frieze (Third Style, with a black ground) discovered in the " Street of Abundance " during the new excavations.

Sometimes, however, we find simpler motifs and the artist makes a more sparing use of ornaments, figure paintings, landscapes and elaborately detailed friezes. In other words, abandoning mannerist methods of decoration, he aims at creating a purely geometric pattern in terms of a skillful balance between masses and colors. Amongst a crowd of mural decorations with a plethora of ornaments we sometimes come on one distinguished by its tasteful sobriety. Such are the murals in the atrium and cubiculum of the small House of the Ceii. Indeed a present-day painter seeking inspiration for the mural decorations of some modern home would find more to learn from the House of the Ceii than from the gaudy walls of the House of Lucretius Fronto.

Thus purely ornamental wall-painting was in high favor. Yet its supremacy did not pass unchallenged either in Rome or in Pompeii. Indeed when, after the spacious vistas of the Second Style, the wall became " blind," opaque, once more, many were quick to protest. For these artists seemed to have repudiated their predecessors' victory over Space, their emancipation from architectural constraints, and the imaginative freedom they had so brilliantly achieved. The result was a reversion to the method of the " open " wall. But now instead of striving to give deep perspective to the architecture, the artists sought, rather, to give an airy lightness to their tracts of color and to flood the openings between the pilasters with light. There was also a return to the use of an upper frieze, usually white and suggesting a limitless horizon. Thus the decorative artists of the Third Style allowed themselves a larger freedom, were less obsessed with ornamentation and—this was their leading characteristic—showed a predilection for those aerial, dreamlike architectural forms which the painters of the last style were to bring down from the frieze to the central panel of the wall. During the last thirty years of Pompeii, the murals of the Fourth Style give the impression of a compromise between decorative and three-dimensional composition. The wall

FOURTH-STYLE SCENOGRAPHIC DECORATION. FROM HERCULANEUM. MUSEO NAZIONALE, NAPLES.

no longer had the so to speak organic character of the architectonic compositions inspired by Hellenistic architecture. When these artists reverted to the use of prospect vistas, their work owed its inspiration to the theater, and to the theater alone.

We are reminded of the fantasy of the Baroque decorators when we contemplate that wall at Herculaneum which is one of the most typical examples of Campanian painting in its fourth, ornate style. Might this not be a *maquette* of the décor designed for some gala performance at a court theater by one of those famous Baroque scenic artists of the 17th century, Ferdinando, Giuseppe or Carlo Bibiena ? Unhappily all that remains of this painting is the upper part (and incomplete at that) of a composition which must have filled the entire wall and we can but guess at the marvellous perspective effects it originally included. Yet fragment though it be, this picture gives us much the same impression as must have been produced on the audience at some court theater when the curtain went up. In fact it brings to mind one of those palaces which arose as if by magic on the stage at the first night of some 18th-century opera. For this mural, like other fourth-style Pompeian paintings, drew its inspiration quite literally from the theater. This is confirmed by the presence of a tragic mask on the *propylaeum*, by the flimsy lightness of the edifice depicted, by the glaring light deliberately projected on the recessive vistas, and also by the draped arch characteristic of a proscenium.

Giving free rein to his zest for ornamentation, the artist has displayed an amazing virtuosity in his handling of arabesques, chasings, gildings and the like. The diversity of motifs is no less impressive: columns, spiral or *caelatae*, medallions adorned with festoons and rosettes, candelabra above the pillars, diversified façades, winged Pegasi, hippocampi and dolphins, perspectives extending over several planes and bathed in dazzling light. No less ingenious is the arrangement of the colors: in the foreground grey-blue and carmine; in the middle ground red, white and grey, and dominant in the background, white. Subdued colors surround the details in bronze or gilt, stressing their metallic sheen.

A comparison of this scene with that in the alcove of the Villa of the Mysteries is instructive. There the architectural features are on a single plane and fantastic, almost dreamlike though they are, have a static effect; whereas the decorations on the wall at Herculaneum are treated as if seen from below (as a theater audience sees the stage sets), the normal angle of vision being displaced. Moreover, the whole scene gives an impression of movement, intensified by the flooding light directed upon the various recessive planes, exactly as is done with stage scenery.

However, this example of the last style, in which Baroque procedures are so evident and the architectural lay-out is so obviously a creation of the artist's fancy, should not blind us to the fact that the chief objective of this last style was the presentation of the big picture in the center of the wall. And this picture, no longer relegated to a sort of water-tight compartment but supported by, and inset in, the surface of the wall, was closely integrated into the over-all decorative composition.

THE GREAT CYCLES

In the essentially decorative compositions the picture was treated as subsidiary to the general lay-out of the wall. On the other hand, in the case of the big figure paintings, the strictly decorative values of the wall space were subordinated to the delineation of a specific scene and subject, religious, heroic or historical as the case might be, and in these the artist gave free rein to his imagination. Such was the conception behind those big cycles of pictures which conjure up for us what their forerunners, the large-scale Greek paintings known as *megalographiae*—not one example of which has survived—must have been. Another interesting feature of these Roman picture sequences is that they are the direct precursors of those magnificent frescos which, centuries later, were to adorn the walls and domes of Italian palaces and churches.

This is an exceptional kind of art, and one which, thanks to its noble inspiration and the brilliant craftsmanship of its exponents, ranks far above the ordinary run of Roman and Pompeian painting. Its finest examples are to be found in two houses at Pompeii: two of those stately mansions in which, during the period between the fall of the Republic and the death of Augustus, the Roman and Campanian aristocracy found a refuge from the brawling politics of city life and the graceless intrusions of the *nouveau riche* business man. This was the golden age of Pompeian painting (the " Second Style "), and its splendid consummation can be seen in such buildings and decorations of the period as have survived.

VILLA OF THE MYSTERIES The great picture sequence in the Villa of the Mysteries is one of the outstanding memorials of Campanian art, both for its religious significance and for its high artistic quality. The Villa itself is situated just outside the town, near one of the gates. It is a handsome building and its spacious rooms and loggias still look out across a smiling countryside of vineyards and orchards, towards the bay. This was the country residence of a patrician family, belonging perhaps to that *Gens Istacidia* whose tomb can still be seen on the road leading from the town to the villa; their town house has not been identified. Judging by the size of the foundations of this elegant retreat and by its numerous amenities, we may assume that the fortunate owners of the Villa of the Mysteries spent much time in it and preferred its quietude to the noisy city life of contemporary Pompeii. It would seem, moreover, that the elegant decorations of the Villa owe much to the enlightened taste of the lady of the house, the *domina*, whose portrait we have most probably in one or other of the female figures painted on the walls. Here, in company with her friends, she could devote herself to the cult of those Dionysiac Mysteries which, though not recognized officially and though celebrated in secret, were the expression of a belief deeply rooted in a large section of the community. Some time in the early phase of the Augustan age the mistress of the house commissioned an artist of genius to decorate her salon, adjoining the marriage chamber, with a series of pictures covering the entire cycle of the Mysteries and illustrating the salient features of the ritual.

THE GREAT FRIEZE OF THE DIONYSIAC MYSTERIES. VILLA OF THE MYSTERIES, POMPEII.

We have here not just one or more independent pictures adorning the center of a wall, but a single, self-contained panoramic scene, spanning like an immense frieze the whole wall space of the living-room. Interrupted only by a window, a small door leading into the marriage chamber, and a larger one giving on to the open loggia and the terrace of a "hanging garden," it contains no less than twenty-nine figures. Almost life-size, they confront us in a room brilliantly lighted from the south and east. Whereas in the other rooms of this house decoration plays a leading part, here the decorative elements framing the picture sequence are, on the contrary, reduced to a simple pattern in the Second Style: a socle, cornice and imitation marble surfaces set off merely by effects of chiaroscuro. The walls are uniformly painted in flat color (vermilion), divided up by strips of green, while the frieze and cornices overhead are in stucco. Thus the ritual pageantry of the Mysteries unfolds itself as a sequence untrammelled

PORTRAIT OF THE DOMINA. VILLA OF THE MYSTERIES, POMPEII.

52

by any plastic element, and the figures move, halt, or form in groups quite independently of any preconceived compositional design or architectural schema. Though in the inner (southern) room this painter displays much skill in creating bold, far-flung perspectives, he refrains here from indulging in any effects of this order, and thus the observer's attention is never distracted from the rite in progress. Deliberately, by indicating no more than a threshold and a strip of floor on which the figures stand or move, he has created the atmosphere of one of those plain, undecorated halls in which the votaries of the cult assembled for their sacred banquets. And the austerity of the setting contributes to the sense of secrecy and mystical emotion imbuing all these scenes.

Where there is no break in the continuity of the wall surface the ritual drama achieves a truly classical unity of time and place. The movements, actions and gaze of all the participants are related to the divine couple, physical and spiritual nucleus of the composition. Such indeed is the underlying unity that it is unbroken even by the angles of the walls. Where an interruption in the wall surface coincides with the end of a ceremony, the figures, spaced out or interposed between the openings of the doors or windows, have a complementary or secondary role. And when, standing back, we have a simultaneous view of the two contiguous walls, we are struck by another indication of this artist's gift for architectonically ordered unity. Not only is the composition structurally coherent but we can discern an over-all rhythm of a special kind embracing all the figures without exception; seated or standing, motionless or moving, they alternate in a perfectly balanced linear harmony.

Between the small door leading to the inner room and the big door of the loggia we see a Roman *matrona* (married woman of the upper class) by herself, whom we may well assume to be the lady of the house. Sumptuously clad, her head draped in a flowing scarf, she wears a necklace, a bracelet and a wedding-ring set with precious stones. A stately, hieratic figure, she is seated in a richly decorated chair. Her head propped on her folded arm, she seems lost in meditation, gazing absently into the middle distance, and there is something in her attitude that makes

THE INITIATE, DETAIL.
VILLA OF THE MYSTERIES, POMPEII.

PORTRAIT OF THE DOMINA, DETAIL. VILLA OF THE MYSTERIES, POMPEII.

THE INITIATRIX, DETAIL. VILLA OF THE MYSTERIES, POMPEII.

TERROR-STRICKEN WOMAN, DETAIL. VILLA OF THE MYSTERIES, POMPEII.

SATYR DRINKING. VILLA OF THE MYSTERIES, POMPEII.

us feel she is not taking any personal part in the ritual of the Mystery. So lifelike is the face and so typically Campanian are the features that we are justified in regarding this as an authentic portrait of the *domina*, of the lady herself who commissioned an artist to adorn the walls of her living-room with a representation of the rites of the orgiastic cult of which she was no doubt an adept and initiate.

With the dignified demeanor of some great lady, hierophant of the new, mystical religion, she is watching the sacramental drama being enacted in her own home. Like many a pious woman of a later day whose whim it was that she should figure in some chapel built at her expense, kneeling before the Madonna and the Saints, this lady wished that her likeness should have a place within the picture sequence of the Mystery.

In any case, whether or not this very room was actually used for the celebration of the rite, we cannot but be conscious of the religious atmosphere pervading the scene and immanent in all these figures, rapt in ecstasy or awe, or treading the measures of the ritual dance around the divine couple, Dionysus and Ariadne.

Interspersed among the young women, neophytes or initiates into the rites of Dionysus, are various mythical figures pertaining to the cult: Satyrs and Sileni, a Panisca (daughter of Pan) and a mysterious winged deity. Young serving-maids and married women also play a part in the ceremony, which culminated in the rite of the *hieros gamos*, the sacred nuptials of Dionysus (Bacchus) and Ariadne, as is indicated by the last scene of the sequence, the " bridal toilet. "

Thus we have here the representation of the complete mystery-play of Dionysus in all its phases, and though the interpretation of certain elements may be problematic, there is no mistaking its general trend and leading themes: the reading of the liturgy, the lustral purification *(lustratio)*, the " Silenus," the " Panisca," the woman struck with panic fear, the unveiling of the *mystica vannus*, the flagellation, the orgiastic dance, the wedding toilet, and, finally, a portrait of the lady commissioning the work.

A richly clad woman is standing erect and motionless on the threshold of the room, listening with the devout attention and reverent awe that befit a neophyte to the reading of the liturgy, which is being recited by a young naked boy in a quavering voice under the direction of a seated matron. The ceremony proper begins with this figure of a woman, who gives the impression of having just emerged from the small door opening off the inner room. Dressed as a bride, she has a slightly studied attitude, with one hand resting on her hip, and is watching the esoteric rites in which she will soon be called on to take part, with the air of a young provincial débutante, at once intrigued and scared by the ordeal before her.

In the next scene, that of the rite of lustral purification, figures a maidservant, a young woman, serene and virginal, with the body and shoulders of an adolescent, her slimness making an effective contrast with the flaccid obesity of the "Singing Satyr" (Silenus), who stands at a short distance from her on the right.

After the lustration, the scene of the drunken, god-possessed Silenus and that of the " Panisca," dainty as a Theocritean shepherdess, we are nearing the action proper of the sacred drama. The woman, who is moving towards the center of the back wall,

GIRL UNDERGOING THE ORDEAL AND BACCHANTE. VILLA OF THE MYSTERIES, POMPEII.

has obviously been gripped by sudden terror. She makes an instinctive movement of retreat but cannot avert her gaze from the horrid fascination of the spectacle before her. Everything in her look and attitude tells of her affright, so dramatically conveyed by the twist of her body, the lips half parted in a muffled scream, the palm of her left hand stretched forth as if to fend off some terrifying vision. So abruptly has she swung round that her *kolpos* has slipped open, uncovering her breast, and her veil, caught in the wind, no longer falls in graceful folds around her head but billows out behind, forming a sort of nimbus. It would seem that the cause of this sudden panic is the glimpse she has just had of the flagellation taking place on the wall confronting her.

Some have held that the scene of Silenus and the two other Satyrs should be interpreted as a magical rite of divination. More probably, in our opinion, that striking group composed of a Satyr with a hideous stage mask and another burying his face in

GIRL UNDERGOING THE ORDEAL, DETAIL. VILLA OF THE MYSTERIES, POMPEII.

THE BRIDAL TOILET, DETAIL. VILLA OF THE MYSTERIES, POMPEII.

a silver bowl, merely illustrates the ceremony of the drinking of the sacramental wine. The young Satyr is greedily drinking from the bowl his seated companion is proffering to him. It probably contains *kykeon*, the sacred drink of the participants in the Orphic Dionysiac mysteries.

Next we have the scene of Dionysus and Ariadne and the unveiling of the *mystica vannus* (mystical winnowing-basket), and, lastly, in the flagellation ceremony comes the culminating point of the ritual. A figure with black wings wide outspread is lashing the victim: this winged figure probably represents the spirit of " Aidos " or " Pudor " which has been outraged by the woman's intention of opening the mystic basket in which the phallus, symbol of male fertility, lies hidden.

The woman seeking initiation had to undergo this " ordeal by beating " before celebration of her mystic wedlock with the god. Such indeed was the rite, at once physical and symbolic, of purification in all times and places of the ancient world. Thus in Arcadia women flogged each other during the Dionysiac festival, and at the Roman Lupercalia women were lashed by the celebrants so as to expel from them the demon of sterility. And in all the phallic or phallophoric rites of the Dionysus cult similar practices obtained. It seems likely that this picture represents the flagellation of a young wife, not yet a mother: in which case the rite of the Luperci, peculiar to Latium, was assimilated here to the rite of Dionysus—or, more accurately, to that of Liber, the old Italian deity identified with the Greek Dionysus as the god of the productivity of nature.

The warm pinkish flesh-tints of the young woman's back and breast tell out against the purplish-brown cloak, and she has sunk her head on the knees of a compassionate matron. It may be that the pain of the ordeal she has undergone, and which perhaps is not yet ended, has made her faint; her eyes are shut and dark rings, like emblems of the shadow of death, encircle them; damp with sweat, her matted hair lies plastered on her forehead. The imploring gaze her friend is casting at the winged figure, and her soothing hand, are of no avail to allay the victim's agony.

After the ordeal comes the mystical marriage. A blond, somewhat fleshy young woman is seated in a chair with elaborately carved legs. Her gracefully molded arms are bedecked with bracelets; she is wearing a flimsy sleeveless chiton and a yellow, violet-bordered mantle held in at the waist by a girdle of a similar color. Like Venus she is attended by a young serving-maid elegant enough to figure in the company of the Graces, and a Cupid is holding up a looking-glass for her to study her reflected self. Human and celestial elements are mingled in this scene and, as in the *Aldobrandini Wedding*, allegorical figures and effigies of divinities are placed beside the wedding bed. Yet in the languid, almost weary gesture of the young bride, in the somewhat over-realistic rendering of the parting of her hair, and in the self-complacent gaze she is casting at the mirror, there are (despite the presence of the little Cupid) too obvious recalls of the everyday life of a lady of fashion, for this woman to be literally identified with any celestial being. On the contrary, we have here a flesh-and-blood young Roman lady who, after undergoing the ordeal, is preparing for the " mystical wedding."

As regards the artistic value of the pictures in the Villa of the Mysteries there is much conflict of opinion. Indeed the judgments of connoisseurs and critics on the originality of the painting we describe as Roman, and in particular that discovered at Pompeii are widely divergent. One wonders, however, if, when confronted by an *ensemble* so self-coherent and displaying such consummate mastery of his craft on the artist's part, we are really justified in raising the issue whether we have here a more or less faithful copy of some famous Greek model of the Hellenistic age, or if this is not, rather, an original creation, the masterwork of a great Campanian painter.

Obviously the depiction of a ritual ceremony, concerned as it necessarily is with certain set figures and themes determined by an ancient rite, can never be a wholly original work. But here the artist reveals a real, very personal genius in the feeling of living, breathing humanity that he has imparted to his figures. For these are far indeed from being mere lay-figures or stereotyped effigies; on the contrary, he has studied the world around him with an observant eye and drawn freely on his personal visual experience. In fact this work admirably illustrates the most original features of Campanian painting: its deliberate break with neo-classical conventions and its tendency to humanize deities and heroes. Thus the Dionysus (in the Dionysus and Ariadne scene), with his puffy face, broad nose and gaze bemused with amorous ecstasy, illustrates the Roman conception of Bacchus, and is quite different from the *Dionysos mystes* of Greek myth. The thick-set Silenus, enraptured by the strains of his own lyre, has a human expression far to seek in the whole Hellenistic repertory of semi-divine figures, while the Panisca and the little Satyr have an almost Puckish sprightliness, racy of the soil, and the drinking Satyr is much like any young Italian peasant.

The same may be said of most of the women painted by this artist; these are not stock figures, but lively, realistic portraits. Let us consider, for example, the charming blond young woman making ready for the marriage bed; her gestures have a naturalness which we should be hard put to it to find in any picture of a Greek gynaeceum, and even the presence of the little Cupid does not detract from the complete realism of the scene. Then, again, how lifelike is that portrait of a woman no longer young, with a rather stolid face, dressed in sumptuous garments that fail to mask the thickness of her figure! And, finally, in the purification scene we have highly effective portraits: the austere profile of the priestess contrasting both with the chubby face of the serving-maid and with the shy grace of the girl pouring the lustral water.

Thus, by frankly discarding the stereotyped procedures of the neo-classicists, this artist, greatly daring, succeeded in giving his figures a direct human appeal and expressing the emotions which are stimulated by participation in a secret rite involving the deepest layers of consciousness and comprising torture and mystic-orgiastic ecstasy.

True, the decoration of the Villa of the Mysteries was the work of an artist trained in the school of Campanian Hellenism and it was from this he took his religious conceptions, themes and figure technique. But he vigorously recast these in the mold of his own personality, and his art is an expression of both the moral and the aesthetic outlook of the sophisticated Roman and Campanian élite of his day.

THE PHILOSOPHER. FROM THE VILLA BOSCOREALE. MUSEO NAZIONALE, NAPLES.

The second great cycle of figural decoration comes from another handsome country house in the Pompeii area. It was discovered in 1900 in the country resort of Boscoreale, not far from the site where (in 1895) a remarkable find of silverware, now in the Louvre, had been made in a rural villa. After the excavations were concluded the Villa Boscoreale was reburied in the earth; its handsome paintings were dispersed, and shared between the Metropolitan Museum, New York, the Museum of Naples and the Louvre. It is much to be regretted that this wonderful *ensemble* of harmoniously planned architectural and decorative elements cannot be seen, as is the case with the Villa of the Mysteries, as an organic whole.

The Villa Boscoreale belongs to the type of aristocratic country residence that became more or less standardized in the first Augustan period; at once rustic and elegant in conception, it comprised a colonnade, entrance hall and central peristyle. The reception rooms were richly adorned with murals, associating the two favorite media of the Second Style: architectural effects and scenes containing figures. The motifs used in the former were new, elaborate and varied. Thus the walls of the peristyle were decorated with huge festoons of flowers and fruits, interspersed with painted columns whose spacing harmonized with that of the real pillars of the peristyle and the openings between them. The painting in a large side room is remarkable for its boldly novel handling of perspective in a view of city streets, with terraced houses full of windows, balconies, porticos and loggias and, dotted amongst them, small shrines of gods and rustic nymphs.

At Boscoreale as in the Villa of the Mysteries the reception room and triclinium contained large figure compositions; here, however, the theme of the picture sequence is not a religious rite but of an historical order. Typical personages of the Hellenistic world figure in it: monarchs, queens and a woman playing the cithara. The gestures and demeanor of these figures, like the costumes, tell of a world which, if not wholly foreign, was far removed from the Roman and Campanian *milieu*. The sumptuous hall of some royal palace furnishes the setting and against the vermilion-red ground of the wall (which is edged by a richly gilded frieze) there rise the smooth shafts of marble columns, ringed with metal bands and decorated with rosettes. There is no means of knowing whom the personages we see in grave confabulation are intended to represent. It would seem the artist had recourse to some iconographic precedent, and one theory is that these persons are Antigonus II, son of King Demetrius Poliorcetes of Macedonia, and his mother Phila. We are, however, more inclined to see in these persons members of the royal court of the Ptolemies of Egypt, then in frequent contact with Campania. In any case we may see in the august, bearded old man, leaning on a twisted staff and gazing pensively at Antigonus and Phila, one of those court philosophers whom royal families attached as teachers to their households.

Such indeed is the majesty the artist has conferred on this remarkable figure that it overshadows all the others. The old man stands well apart from them, at the far end of a wall, and the grave aloofness of his mien strikes an effective contrast with the effeminate young prince and the portly matron seated in a chair; hiding beneath the ample folds of his huge cloak the signs of poverty that were the normal attributes of the wandering Greek sage, he seems a noble embodiment of the ripe wisdom of ancient Hellas. We certainly have here the likeness of one of the great thinkers of the Hellenistic age, and some have identified him with Menedemus of Eretria, a distinguished member of the School of " Moderate Cynics." In this portrait the artist has achieved a truly wonderful spiritualization of his subject; indeed of all the many portraits of Greek philosophers, in marble or bronze, that have come down to us, none shows a keener psychological insight. Everything in this portrait is apposite, and perfect of its kind. The cloak has the folds and undulations we find in the statues of orators and sages executed in the purest Hellenistic style, while the face has the look of shrewd, penetrating observation characteristic of the finest Hellenistic portraits. The painter has used a brush heavily charged with color and the texture of the pigment is brought out by the brushstrokes, the result being that a curious vibrancy seems to pervade this figure, statuesque though it be. One has a feeling that the old man with the staff is, as it were, keyed up; fretting with impatience to move forward and enter into conversation with the young prince and his royal mother.

If we compare the Boscoreale artist's work with that of the painter of the Villa of the Mysteries, we find that he achieves a far more finished style in rendering the personalities and idiosyncrasies of his historic figures. Above all, he shows a greater skill in depicting garments, in dealing with which the painter of the Mysteries betrayed a certain lack of proficiency. Nothing in the execution of these figures reveals the handiwork of a specifically Campanian artist. Even the features of that woman playing the cithara (whom some have plausibly enough thought to be the lady of the house) are treated with a realism very different from that of the matron and the bride in the Villa of the Mysteries. The very subject—figures of the rulers in a royal palace—suggests that the artist was a Greek master familiar with the Hellenistic world and with the still surviving traditions of the Eastern Dynasts.

BASILICA OF HERCULANEUM   The famous Villa of the Papyri at Herculaneum contained no works of pictorial art in any way comparable with the bronze and marble statuary discovered there. On the other hand the Basilica near the forum of the city (as yet only partially excavated) has given us a considerable number of paintings. Executed on the concave surfaces of niches giving on the interior of the great hall they depict episodes of classical mythology: the centaur Chiron instructing young Achilles, Marsyas teaching Olympos to play the flute, and—conceived on a larger scale both as to actual size and compositional development—the scenes of Hercules finding Telephus in Arcadia, and Theseus' return from his victorious encounter with the Minotaur. It is not yet known exactly how these large-scale pictures (" megalographies ") were integrated into the over-all mural decorative scheme, but one thing is clear: that they were the work of a painter of the early Flavian period, who, while making the utmost realism his aim, tended to give his figures the rhythm, volume and relief of late Hellenistic statuary. An inscription records that the Basilica was erected thanks to the generosity of Marcus

THESEUS TRIUMPHANT, DETAIL. FROM THE BASILICA OF HERCULANEUM. MUSEO NAZIONALE, NAPLES.

Nonius Balbus, Proconsul, the most eminent and wealthiest citizen of Herculaneum. In a sort of sanctuary within the Basilica were placed statues of the Emperor and his family, while two equestrian statues of the Proconsul flanked the main entrance. It seems probable that some famous artist from the neighboring city of Neapolis was called in to make the wall-paintings, since many large schools of sculptors, bronze-workers and painters are known to have flourished in that city—as is evidenced by the fact that the orator Philostratus (in the 2nd century of the Empire) thought fit to draw up a *catalogue raisonné* of the numerous pictures on view at the civic picture-gallery (Pinacotheca) of Naples. Moreover, the paintings in the Basilica do not suggest the work of any local school; rather, they bring to mind a type of painting that may well have developed in a highly cultured center such as Naples, where in the first century of the Empire, under the Claudian and Flavian dynasties, there was such vast enthusiasm for literature and the arts.

In the large composition depicting Hercules and Telephus the artist's originality is most evident in the subsidiary figures and motifs. Thus, though the depiction of Arcadia is cold and academic and though the hero's face is brutal, almost repulsive, there is much playfulness in the artist's rendering of the little Satyr with the pan-pipes and shepherd's crook; indeed this boy's face has all the naturalness of the Satyrs in the Villa of the Mysteries, while, similarly, the doe suckling Telephus reminds us of the " Panisca's " fawn. Also, the detail of the basket of golden grapes ranks high amongst the many still lifes figuring in the murals at Pompeii and Herculaneum.

In the *Theseus Triumphant* reminiscences of plastic art are even more in evidence; the hero's solidly balanced stance and massive strength obviously recall some work of sculpture which the artist used as his model. The allegorical forms personifying Crete, the grateful children trying to kiss the hero's hand and the monster prone in the shadows at his feet play only subsidiary roles; the statuesque form of Theseus dominates the whole composition. The broad red, evenly applied brushstrokes with which Theseus' body is rendered, dappled with touches of shadow here and there to show the play of muscles, contribute to this statuesque effect; similarly the head, painted in vibrant touches with sudden gleams of light, has the plastic vigor of sculptured bronze. Energy and an indomitable will are conveyed by the hero's expression, and the sense of contained power emanating from this noble head, crowned with unruly locks, is singularly impressive.

In commenting on these paintings analogies have sometimes been traced with the Baroque style of Pergamum; thus it has been suggested that their grandiose effect is largely due to the artist's extravagant modeling and rhetorical exaggerations; that, in short, the *Telephus* definitely recalls the bas-reliefs of the famous Altar of Zeus, and the *Theseus Triumphant* is merely sculpture transposed into another medium. Actually, these works might quite as well be likened to certain altarpieces of the early Seicento, and we are almost tempted to see a family likeness between the paintings in the Basilica and the magniloquent (but academically correct) forms and procedures of Neapolitan painting.

THE ALEXANDER MOSAIC. FROM THE HOUSE OF THE FAUN, POMPEII. MUSEO NAZIONALE, NAPLES.

There is a quite unique interest in this famous mosaic depicting the Battle of Issus (by which name also it is known), since all we know of large-scale Greek painting is by hearsay and what we have here is evidently an exceptionally faithful copy of one of the great masterpieces of Greek painting in the 4th century B.C. This mosaic, which was employed as a pavement, belongs to the kind known as *opus vermiculatum* in which very small tesserae were used, enabling the artist to blend his colors smoothly and produce effects of chiaroscuro. Indeed the Alexander Mosaic, which originally figured in the pavement of the House of the Faun at Pompeii, has the texture of a finely woven carpet; the vertical position given it in the Naples Museum—like a picture on the wall—is justified by its exceptional artistic value and the fact that its original was thus displayed. Stemming undoubtedly from some great center of mosaic art—Alexandria in Egypt or some cultural center in one of the Aegean islands—it was probably brought to Pompeii during the " golden age " of second-style decoration, when large compositions with figures had a great vogue. In very early times this mosaic underwent some ill-advised " restorations " by a Pompeian mosaicist; we can see his handiwork in the different quality of the tesserae employed and the clumsy patching-up of certain gaps on the left of the composition. The discovery of this mosaic on October 24, 1831, caused quite a sensation, indeed it was a red-letter day in the annals of the excavations at Pompeii.

The subject depicted is the Battle of Issus (in Cilicia) which took place in 333 B.C. and in which Alexander the Great routed the Persian king Darius. The artist has picked on the most dramatic moment of the conflict, when, the tide of battle having turned in Alexander's favor, the two leaders, victor and vanquished, confronted each other in the thick of the *mêlée*. Skillfully contrasted are the fiery energy of the young Macedonian and the defeated Persian's air of mournful resignation. This theme became a great favorite with painters, and claims to have been the first to use it were advanced for Aristides of Thebes, Philoxenus of Eretria and Helena of Alexandria (daughter of Timon of Egypt), amongst others. Thus here we have not only the most ancient battlepiece in art, but also one of the most remarkable achievements in this field.

The background is quite flat, there is no trace of landscape except for a tree shattered as though struck by lightning, and no change of color differentiates the ground from the horizon. Thus the spectator's attention is focused wholly on the clash of the opposing armies. Wearing the massive yellow Persian tiara and flowing robes, Darius is fleeing in his chariot, whereas Alexander is bareheaded and clad in armor. His eyes aglow, his hair streaming in the wind like a young god's, he is charging through the battling crowd and lunging forward to drive his lance through a Persian who is trying to impede his onslaught on the fleeing monarch. A hedge of the long spears called *sarissae* has been formed around Darius' chariot to cover his retreat, while in the foreground Persian horsemen and their steeds are being cut down by the Greeks.

Even in this copy we can feel that the artist who painted the original picture was deeply moved both by the dramatic significance of this momentous clash between the Greek world and the Orient, and by the heroism of the two protagonists, the young King of Macedonia and the great eastern potentate. It is on this center of interest that the whole composition converges: on Alexander pressing forward with reckless courage, having no eyes for anything except his retreating foe, and on Darius looking back on his wounded captains, with anguish in his face. The headlong confusion of the rout is skillfully conveyed by the fallen weapons and armor strewing the battlefield.

Though there are no specific indications of the space dimension, the artist has suggested it indirectly by the arrangement of the lances fretting the skyline, by overlapping figures admirably suggesting the serried tumult of the battle, by a dextrous gradation of tones, and finally by some well-contrived foreshortenings in the forms of the combatants and those of horses wildly plunging or felled to the ground.

Here, as in those elegant vignettes signed Dioskourides of Samos in the so-called Villa of Cicero at Pompeii, the colors (red, brown, black, white and occasionally yellow) are subdued, and the subtle handling of tones calls to mind a very finely woven tapestry. It may be that, when interpreting the original painting, the mosaicist simplified and toned down the colors; but perhaps we would do better to assume that he deliberately restricted himself to the four colors which alone (so Pliny assures us) were used by the greatest masters of Greek painting in their most famous works.

4
PICTURES WITH FIGURE-SUBJECTS
EPIC THEMES

When Encolpius, the most cultivated of the three disreputable heroes of Petronius' *Satiricon*, inquired, on entering Trimalchio's home, what the painted decorations were supposed to represent, he was told that they were scenes from the Iliad and the Odyssey, with a gladiatorial contest thrown in. Trimalchio, a millionaire plebeian, had made his home—it was there that he gave his famous Rabelaisian banquet—in some seaside town of Campania, almost certainly Pozzuoli. What we learn from Petronius (through the mouth of Encolpius) about Trimalchio's mansion is corroborated by the finds in numerous houses at Pompeii, but with this difference: that whereas Trimalchio chose his showy pictures with a view to masking his abysmal ignorance, at Pompeii, on the contrary, the mural paintings in those elegant, patrician homes vouch for their owners' enlightened appreciation of the greatest of all Epics.

It was in the course of the excavation of the so-called House of the Tragic Poet, in 1824 or 1825, that Pompeian painting at its splendid best was brought to light. For, small though it is, this house is unequaled for the excellence and variety of the figure-compositions which covered the walls of the atrium, the peristyle and the triclinium. At least five of these paintings deal with epic themes, and thus, by virtue of their style and subject-matter, tend to throw light on the vexed question of the relation between the Greek originals and their Campanian " copies. " These are *The Sacrifice of Iphigenia*, *The Departure of Chryseis*, *The Obduracy of Agamemnon*, *The Wrath of Achilles and the Surrendering of Briseis* and *The Marriage of Hera and Zeus on Mount Ida*. Later on, other outstanding works on epic themes were discovered; amongst them *Achilles in Scyros* (in the House of the Dioscuri) and *Thetis with Hephaestus* (in the House of Siricus). Pictures dealing with the same themes, of varying stylistic merit, have also been found in other houses.

Besides these pictures, there existed other large-scale figure-paintings of Homeric themes, for example the composition in the portico of the Temple of Apollo, unfortunately lost to us today, and several narrative friezes illustrating in serial order the leading episodes of the Iliad and providing one might almost say an illustrated version of the poem. Excavations carried out in the last few decades have brought to light some of these friezes deriving from the *Tabulae Iliacae*.

In the House of the Lararium a frieze in white stucco on a blue ground depicts the fight to the death between Hector and Achilles, and the dramatic meeting of Priam and Achilles, when the former pleaded for the dead body of his son. In the House of the Cryptoporticus (also called the Homeric House) no less than fifty scenes from the Iliad—some twenty of which have survived—were aligned along the wall in separate panels. In the House of Loreius Tiburtinus the frieze in the triclinium illustrates several episodes from the last books of the Iliad, to which some legends of Latin origin are annexed. In the House of Menander a triptych covering three walls depicts crucial incidents of the siege and burning of Troy: *The Death of Laocoön, The Wooden Horse, The Burning of Priam's Palace.*

Pompeian painting, it would seem, took over the great Homeric themes as represented in classical works that had found their way to Rome and in more or less free interpretations of them by Greek and Roman copyists. This is borne out by Pliny who, in a brief but enlightening note, speaks of a whole cycle of paintings of the Iliad in the portico of Philippus at Rome, the work of one Theoros or Theon of Samos. Further proof is the existence at Pompeii of numerous paintings on these same themes which differ from one another rather in their stylistic and formal qualities than in their general approach to the subject. In fact all these pictures reflect the compositional lay-out of the classical paintings and bas-reliefs of the 4th century B.C. The scene of action is usually an interior, sketchily indicated by a few architectural details or by the general " atmosphere." The figures fill almost the entire picture space and are arranged on successive planes in depth and height. Placed in the center and well to the fore, and painted in more vivid colors, the protagonists stand out against the subsidiary figures. Thus they are invested with an heroic dignity and this classical treatment of the leading figures probably derives from Greek originals or works closely resembling these. The secondary, episodic figures, on the other hand, have a more direct and human appeal; the artist displays a greater freedom of execution, and we feel that he has followed his own bent and broken with the time-honored formulas.

We need not linger on the somewhat over-praised *Sacrifice of Iphigenia* from the House of the Tragic Poet, in which the very real grief we see on the face of Agamemnon hardly suffices to redeem the frigid academicism of the composition as a whole. We shall consider, rather, those works in which the stylistic qualities of the originals may still be discerned, the sequence relating to the exploits of Achilles: *Achilles in Scyros, The Making of Achilles' Arms in Hephaestus' Forge,* and *The Obduracy of Agamemnon.*

Much may be learnt from a study of *Achilles in Scyros*; we have the good fortune to possess two versions of the picture, one from the House of the Dioscuri which, though fragmentary, is remarkable for its style and well-ordered composition; the other, complete, but loosely constructed, was found in a house in Region 9. This was accompanied by two other pictures showing the preparations for the forging of Achilles' weapons and the hero carrying them away. Incomplete though it is, the version in the House of the Dioscuri suffices not only to give us an idea of the great beauty of the Greek original, but also to appreciate the fine artistic sensitivity of the Pompeian painter.

Disguised in female dress in the palace of King Lycomedes of Scyros, Achilles is "exposed" by Ulysses and Diomedes, who have cunningly excited the fighting instinct of the young hero by the sight and sound of arms. The painting illustrates the dramatic

ACHILLES IN SCYROS. FROM THE HOUSE OF THE DIOSCURI, POMPEII. MUSEO NAZIONALE, NAPLES.

moment when Achilles, having betrayed himself, is about to make his escape. Still in the dress of a maiden, he is hesitating, but already his hand is on his sword and the look on his face tells of his ardor for the fray. Panic-stricken, Deidameia is fleeing from the room, while her father, King Lycomedes, watches what is happening in helpless bafflement.

The dramatic quality of this scene, which is located in a plain architectural setting painted in cold hues, is stressed by the vivid, almost strident colors, though here and there a gentler note is struck by the blue-grey nuances of the women's garments. Achilles' hair is copper-colored and his eyes are flashing. His youthful form, glimpsed in the billowing confusion of his flimsy garments, strikes a contrast with the stalwart bulk of Ulysses and Diomedes. Metallic glints accentuate the arms, legs and face of Ulysses, who is bearded and wears a Phrygian cap, and the artist has deliberately played these off against the soft pink flesh-tints of Deidameia. Similar contrasts and harmonies are to be found in another famous picture, *The Surrendering of Briseis*, in which the composition, with its lavish use of contrasting effects, seems even more accomplished. Achilles and Patroclus are shown one in front view and the other with his back to us, while the form of Briseis, wrapped in her mantle, a look of anguish on her face, tells out against the warriors' armor and the opening of the tent. The finely chiseled features of the old man, Phoenix, call to mind one of those superb portraits of Greek sages and philosophers many of which have, happily, survived.

Amidst these scenes of epic combat and the clash of arms, an exquisite fragment of another picture found in the House of the Tragic Poet strikes a gentler note. A shy, charming young girl is boarding a ship; this is Chryseis, whom Agamemnon, at Apollo's bidding, is sending back to her father. The colors are appropriate to this scene of leave-taking which, if equally romantic, has not the dramatic character of Achilles' departure from Scyros. The tranquil light that hovers on the sea is suggested by passages of grey and violet, while the girl's dress is rendered in delicate nuances. A sailor's obvious eagerness to do her service and the unabashed curiosity of a young boy standing near make an effective foil to Chryseis' maidenly reserve. Her gaze reflects her natural anxiety at the long sea voyage before her and her misgivings as to her return.

In all the noble compositions in the House of the Tragic Poet, the House of the Dioscuri and the House of Siricus, the pictures on Homeric themes still drew inspiration from the great classical painting of the 4th century B.C. But such themes soon found their way into the normal repertory of painters, thanks largely to the wide diffusion of the *Tabulae Iliacae*, and also to the fact that interest was developing in the legends connected with Aeneas' flight from Troy and the founding of Rome. Thus, aside from these works executed in the classical heroic spirit, there were others catering for tastes of a less exalted order, in which the painter gave rein to his own creative imagination. With the result that a kind of " popularized " Iliad made its appearance on the walls of some Pompeian houses.

A case in point is the triptych, mentioned above, in the House of Menander, which is a typical re-interpretation of an epic theme on the lines of a popular legend.

The three pictures it contains are painted in bright colors, the composition is well balanced, and the artist displays an engaging spontaneity as well as an instinctive gift for narrative in his transmutation of epic grandeur into the likeness of a fairy-tale. This is very noticeable in the scene in Priam's palace, the panel in the best state of preservation. Two dramatic incidents are taking place simultaneously in a room of the palace, which is already invaded by the smoke of the burning city. One is the meeting of Menelaus and Helen in the presence of the defeated Trojans, and the other, Ajax laying hold of Cassandra, who has sought sanctuary under the statue of Athena. In the center, disarmed and quaking with fear, the aged Priam is vainly trying to save his favorite daughter.

By including two episodes in the same picture, and visualizing the tragic helplessness of Priam forced to witness the humiliation of Cassandra, the painter has imparted great dramatic tension to his work. The colors, too, are highly effective, particularly

THE TROJAN HORSE. FROM POMPEII. MUSEO NAZIONALE, NAPLES.

striking being the vivid contrasts between Menelaus' flashing armor and Helen's half-naked body, and between the massive strength of Ajax and the pale, swooning Cassandra. Royal insignia, crimson robes and a scepter add dignity and nobility to the pathetic figure of the hapless King of Troy.

When, breaking with the traditional lay-out of the classical repertory, these painters fell to bodying forth their personal conception of such scenes, as in the "Landscapes of the Odyssey," they developed a modernity of expression and an imaginative range that are nothing short of amazing. Let us take as an example a painting, also from Pompeii, whose theme is one that constantly recurs in ancient art: the Trojan Horse.

The confusion, the wild jubilation of the Trojan populace, and the glow of torch-light are rendered in quite the impressionist manner. Escorted by a throng of warriors and citizens, the horse is being dragged into Troy under cover of night. The walls and towers of the city loom dimly on the horizon and the sky is lit up by the glare of torches. Like an omen of impending catastrophe, the form of a woman is seen above the doomed city; she is rushing forward like an avenging Fury, brandishing a lighted torch. In the middle distance, between the walls and the procession, soldiers are advancing in serried ranks: an almost formless mass of hooded men, vague shapes outlined against the surrounding darkness, and distinguishable only by the halberds pointing up above the ranks. In the foreground is a little group of men, buffeted and half-blinded by the glare of the torches, straining every muscle to drag the ponderous horse which, stiffly erect, with its forelegs planted in the soil, seems to resist their efforts. An awestruck crowd brings up the rear, while in front, between a ragged, twisted tree and the statue of Athena, we see Cassandra, full of dire forebodings, hurrying forward. Some minor figures, briefly indicated by wavering streaks of light, heighten the effect of feverish activity. Mallet in hand, a carpenter seems to be tinkering with one of the legs of the horse, while another man, a little way off, his movements limned in light, seems to be directing operations and urging the others on. At the foot of the column is a seated woman, whose placid form acts as a counterpoise to the straining, slanting bodies of the men dragging the wooden horse.

Here landscape and narrative are fully integrated. And we can gauge the skill of this local painter who, with the technical procedures brought to the fore in our day by the Impressionists, imparted such tragic grandeur to this night-piece and organized his highlights to such superb effect. Quite likely he was drawing on his actual experience of the illuminations and night fêtes that took place periodically at Pompeii, and these he sublimated on to the plane of the ancient myth—which perhaps is why this strange picture gives the impression of a scene of real life, poetically interpreted by a gifted artist.

GODS, HEROES, MYTHS AND SACRED RITES

When Pompeii became a Roman colony (in 80 B.C.) it was placed under the patronage of Venus, and named Colonia Veneria Cornelia, this last epithet being a tribute to L. Cornelius Sulla, the dictator, who had conquered the city. One of its handsomest temples was dedicated to the goddess of love. When this temple was destroyed, a start was made with rebuilding it, but the work was never completed. Up to the present, indeed, no bronze or marble statue of Venus has been discovered on this site. Thus no material evidence would have been forthcoming of the " official " local cult of this goddess, were it not for the numerous wall-paintings that have survived. Venus is, in fact, their most favored subject and figures not only on the walls of houses, in *atria*, in dining-rooms, in *cubicula*, but also in gardens and on shop-fronts. In the pictures with mythological themes and motifs she is treated in the classical convention, whereas in those of more clearly religious inspiration we see her under a more human, less formal aspect. In both cases, however, the Venus of Pompeii is far from being that vision of idealized beauty with which classical art has familiarized us. Often she has the somewhat provincial cast of face and attitude of some comely woman of Campania; elsewhere she cuts an hieratic figure, draped in an austerely cut *stola* and carrying the attributes of her godhead.

For the sophisticated, somewhat licentious Pompeians, with their propensity for romantico-idyllic literature and the witty epigrams of the Alexandrian poets, the depiction of Venus was a welcome pretext for elegant artistry, with an emphasis on the erotic aspects of her legend. Thus we have Venus chastising Cupid (as in that charming little picture *Cupid Punished*) or insidiously prompting Helen to be unfaithful to her husband (House of the Priest Amandus), Venus in love ministering to the wounded Adonis (House of Adonis), Venus the peace-maker disarming Mars (House of Mars and Venus)—this, incidentally, was a subject of which Pompeian painters were particularly fond—or, again, the meeting of the divine pair in some local gynaeceum. In this last instance there is no question of a mere liaison; we are shown what amounts to an official marriage ceremony. It is the theme of a small panel that can still be seen, in the full splendor of its original color, in the House of Lucretius Fronto. An almost exact replica of this has been discovered in a house in the district which is now being excavated.

Wrapped in a mantle, Venus is seated, with the gravely meditative air of a young bride, in a room with big windows overlooking a peristyle. It is a bedroom, as is proved by the couch draped in a rich fabric and thickly cushioned. Standing beside the goddess, Mars (Ares) wears a blue chlamys and a crested helmet. He is trying to bare the goddess' breast, but demurely she restrains him; in fact she reminds us far more of a well-bred Roman lady than of the laughter-loving Aphrodite. A winged Cupid is in attendance, and the two serving-maids on the right seem to be waiting for an order from their mistress to proceed with the " wedding toilet " of the bride. Two other maids are to be seen behind the couch, beside a man with a winged forehead, deeply

THE COURTSHIP OF VENUS AND MARS. HOUSE OF MARCUS LUCRETIUS FRONTO, POMPEII.

tanned skin and watchful gaze. Some have identified him with Hermes, the winged messenger who was presently to bring tidings to Hephaestus of the capture of the lovers in a golden net; but he may be merely some benevolent deity, such as Hypnos or Hymenaeus. This charming *scène galante* of antiquity would not have looked out of place in the boudoir of some fashionable 18th-century Parisienne.

ANDROMEDA AND PERSEUS. FROM POMPEII. MUSEO NAZIONALE, NAPLES.

But Venus was not the only deity favored by artists in quest of themes featuring romantic love; they often painted other members of the hierarchy of Olympus. Jupiter, for instance, in the toils of his complicated love-affairs with Europa, Io and Danaë; Apollo, unable to choose between Danaë and Cyparissus ; Poseidon and Amphitrite; Diana's love for Endymion and Actaeon's ill-starred glimpse of her when bathing.

THE CENTAURS IN THE PALACE OF PIRITHOUS. FROM POMPEII. MUSEO NAZIONALE, NAPLES.

This fabulous world of heroes and amorous adventures was a godsend for our painters, and we find an aura of romanticism clinging to all their pictures, whose basic theme was love's ineluctable dominion over the hearts of men and gods. Thus Hercules is not merely the benevolent hero, slayer of monsters; he is also love's victim and its henchman. We find him brutally avenging Deianira for the violence done her by the Centaur Nessus (House of the Centaur), abducting Auge when (like Nausicaa) she was washing garments, and by whom, unawares, he had a son, Telephus, whom he subsequently recognized; acquiring more by " blarney " than by force the golden apples of the Hesperides (House of the Priest Amandus); or, again, half-drunk, making an exhibition of himself in the home of Omphale (House of Marcus Lucretius and House of Siricus). Theseus' famous victory over the Minotaur (Basilica of Herculaneum) had an inglorious sequel in his desertion of Ariadne (House of the Tragic Poet) and this theme of the lovely, hapless victim marooned on the desert island from which Dionysus rescued her, was very popular with Campanian painters.

Like a knight-errant of the age of chivalry, Perseus saved the fair Andromeda from the jaws of a sea-monster, and a large picture dealing with this incident was found in the House of the Dioscuri. Its special interest is that it is thought to be one of the most accurate reproductions we possess of a Greek original, in this case probably a work by the Athenian Nikias, a contemporary of Praxiteles. In fact the strong modeling of the bodies, whose bright colors tell out against the rocks and the expanse of sea, bears out what we are told about Nikias' exceptional skill in rendering volumes. None the less the mannered academicism of the figures of the hero and heroine in this picture detracts from its appeal. In helping Andromeda down the rock Perseus has the elegant deportment of a *chevalier servant*, while she manifests a studied propriety quite unsuitable to the occasion. Thus we are inclined to prefer to this much-belauded work a smaller picture (though not so well preserved), in which the artist gives a new, poetic interpretation of this hackneyed theme. This picture has the charm of a hasty, happily inspired sketch; gestures and faces are expressive and the softly tinted air enveloping earth, sea and sky bathes the landscape in shimmering light.

Nor did the Pompeian artists neglect the hapless or malefic heroines of Greek mythology, whose tragic misadventures figured so often on the Greek and Latin stage: Medea, sorceress and murderer of her children, Iphigenia about to be sacrificed to Artemis and carried off to the land of the Tauri—pictures whose originals are ascribed to Timomachus of Byzantium—or, again, Phaedra maddened by Hippolytus' rejection of her love, the tragedy of Alcestis giving her life to save Admetus, the barbarous punishment meted out to Dirce. But, besides these tragic themes, romantic love-stories of the legendary past, such as Hylas ravished by the Nymphs, Phrixos and Helle, Hero and Leander, Pyramus and Thisbe, were in high favor.

In his renderings of mythological themes the painter often had to face the problem of illuminating scenes taking place indoors—a problem which he usually solved by placing windows in the walls or depicting arcades with light streaming between the columns. We have an interesting illustration of the artists' inventiveness in this field

DIANA THE HUNTRESS. FROM STABIAE. MUSEO NAZIONALE, NAPLES.

" PRIMAVERA. " FROM STABIAE. MUSEO NAZIONALE, NAPLES.

SACRIFICE TO DIONYSUS. FROM HERCULANEUM. MUSEO NAZIONALE, NAPLES.

in the picture of the reception of the Centaurs in the palace of Pirithous, on the occasion of his marriage with Hippodamia, daughter of one of the Lapithae. Hippodamia, Pirithous and a terrified child are standing in the vestibule, which is flooded with light streaming in from all directions. The alarming, half-human wedding guests are massed on the threshold and we see an aged Centaur, with a basket of fruit in front of him, his gift to the bride, kissing his host's hand with a courteous gesture that seems to vouch for his good intentions. But we are made to feel that between the group of young Centaurs, waiting stiffly erect, with their heads craned forward, behind the almost grotesque-looking old Centaur bowing to Pirithous on the one hand and, on the other, the nervous woman and timid child, a tension is already developing and its effect is enhanced by the all-pervading luminosity of the air; we *know* that presently the Centaurs will fling themselves savagely upon the bride and the women of the Lapithae.

Deities, heroines and allegorical figures are also to be seen in the formal, highly stylized works used to decorate the alcoves of bedrooms and *exedrae* (niches with stone seats); these reflect the style and manner of the neo-Attic artists.

Noteworthy amongst the various decorations that have been detached from the houses at Stabiae are four small paintings on green or blue grounds, depicting women's figures. The subjects are Diana the Huntress, Leda with the swan, Medea lost in somber musings, and a young woman picking flowers. The figures are painted in light colors, soft nuances of white and yellow, and the delicacy of the brushwork reminds us of encaustic painting on marble. Nothing is added to define the setting, and only a faintly undulating line indicates the ground on which the figures stand or move. For Diana and Medea the artist uses a sky-blue background; for the other two figures, a smooth sea-green expanse.

CENTAUR WITH APOLLO AND AESCULAPIUS. FROM POMPEII. MUSEO NAZIONALE, NAPLES.

YOUNG PRIESTESS. FROM POMPEII. MUSEO NAZIONALE, NAPLES.

Represented as a modest young woman, and recalling the charming women's figures in scenes of the gynaeceum, Diana wears a chiton and a flowing mantle reaching to the ankles, not her light hunting garment, short and held in at the waist. The only attributes of her function that she carries are a bent bow and a single arrow; but so slender is the bow and so unhurried her gait, that she looks more like a citharaedus than like the Goddess of the Hunt.

Medea is resting a sheathed sword upon her arm. With knitted brows and lips wryly twisted she is brooding over the hideous project she has conceived: of killing her children to revenge herself on Jason. Her tragic expression is the same as that in the Herculaneum *Medea*, which is believed, probably rightly, to be a faithful replica of the celebrated *Medea* of Timomachus.

In contrast with Leda, with dark rings under her eyes and embracing the swan with sensual ardor, the *Primavera* is all dainty charm, etherial as the princess in some old-world fairy-tale. Indeed, this young girl picking flowers looks more like an allegorical figure than a real human being. She seems to tread on air and the position—with her back to us—in which she is represented heightens, curiously enough, the effect of idealization, since the fact that all we can see of her head is a slender neck, golden hair and the graceful oval of a cheek, leaves us free to conjure up a vision of the delicate beauty of the unseen face. She is wearing a sleeveless chiton falling low on her right arm and across the gossamer-thin fabric, fluttering in the air as she moves forward, we glimpse the young grace of her body. Lightly she glides across the green meadow, holding in one hand a basket of flowers and turning to pick with the other a frond of small pink blossoms.

YOUNG PRIEST OF ISIS. FROM THE TEMPLE OF ISIS, POMPEII. MUSEO NAZIONALE, NAPLES.

WOMAN'S HEAD. NEW EXCAVATIONS, STABIAE.

In a general way the smaller pictures we shall now consider derived from votive bas-reliefs and since in such cases the painter had no color-scheme to guide him, he tended to stress effects of chiaroscuro in his figures, almost as if he were trying to reproduce the plastic qualities of his model. Amongst the most significant examples of this class of pictures is a panel representing a sacrifice, which reproduces even in its dimensions the lay-out of a votive bas-relief. A god is seated on a throne, and we can identify him as Dionysus more by reason of his cup and thyrsus than by his physical appearance. Garlanded and clad in sumptuous chitons flounced at the waist, three women are carrying offerings. One of them is placing a crown on the god's head, while in her other hand she holds the ritual dish. The other two women seem to be in waiting. On the extreme left a patch of color sketchily indicates a little girl: the child bearing offerings who always figured in votive bas-reliefs. Here a minimum of linework is used for indicating faces, attitudes and movements.

The style and composition of another votive picture, likewise recalling neo-Attic bas-reliefs, was found in the House of Adonis at Pompeii, which owes its name to a big painting on the garden wall. In that picture, which shows Venus and the Cupids succoring Adonis, wounded by a boar, it is obvious that both composition and style derive from some good classical model. But in the small picture which we reproduce an original in the neo-Attic style has been freely interpreted in the new impressionist manner. Its subject is thought to refer to the cult of the *dii salutares*.

A young Centaur with the hind quarters and legs of a colt, his torso bare and his locks floating in the wind, occupies the center of the picture. Holding in one hand a shepherd's staff and in the other a spray of flowers, he cuts a proud and stately figure. On one side is Apollo, recognizable by the *omphalos* beside him and by his posture, that of the classical Apollo Lyceius, the type brought into favor by Praxiteles. There is also a bearded man, usually identified as Aesculapius, sitting near a pedestal on which is a tripod. The central figure is probably the wise Centaur Chiron, expert *inter alia* in the lore of medicine. It is interesting to see here how the composition, despite its classical purity of line, is as it were revivified by the artist's impressionist spontaneity.

Alongside these themes drawn from the lore of gods and heroes, we have representations of sacred rites, which testify to the deep religious sentiments of the young priestesses and their assistants. An illustration is the picture here reproduced of a young woman, which probably formed part of a large composition depicting some religious ceremony. She is wearing a plain, sleeveless, greenish-grey chiton with a red-brown scarf looped round her waist—an attire permitting entire freedom of movement. She is holding some object related to the ceremony; it looks like a small table with carved legs, presumably the table on which the offerings were to be placed. On her head she wears a freshly plucked garland. Her look of anxious attention and bowed head, no less than the droop of her shoulders due to the effort of carrying the sacred utensil with suitable decorum, make it clear she is a priestess and not just a serving-maid in a gynaeceum; in fact she recalls the young woman pouring libations in the Villa of the Mysteries. The composition here is governed by the continuous line of the bending body, the undulating movement of the garment, and the slow, short steps the girl is taking, encumbered as she is by the sacred object she is going to set down beside the altar.

Despite the fact that this scene depicts some religious rite, it too is treated in the new impressionistic manner. Whereas the neo-Attic painters tended to stylize such themes, we have here the free technique and bold use of color typical of the Campanian painter—the transmutation of visual experience into a pure color-impression.

Very different from the idealized *Young Priestess*, with her graceful poise and tranquil, meditative air, is the *Woman's Head*, recently discovered at Stabiae. The woman's hair is streaming in tangled confusion over her breast and shoulders; her lips are parted, she seems to be gasping for breath. Only in the most emotive figures in the Villa of the Mysteries do we find such expressive power. This is only a small fragment and, exceptionally, we have enlarged the original in our reproduction so as to bring out the intense vitality of the drawing, the subtle nuances of color, the interplay of light and shadow in the face, and the rich, warm hues of the hair. We have no clue to the exact nature of the scene in which this woman figured, but there can be no doubt that here we have a young initiate into one of the secret cults, in the throes of mystical emotion. For no ordinary emotion can account for that air of having lost track of the outside world, and tense expectancy.

Striking an exceptional note amongst so many priestesses dressed in the classical manner, whose forms are idealized in deference to their sacred functions, are a group of men and women whose costumes and demeanor show them to be the priests and priestesses of Isis. There was a temple of this goddess in Pompeii, and small shrines devoted to her cult were installed in many private houses. On the walls of the portico of the temple, in which the procession known as the Pompa Isidis took place, were painted a series of Egyptian scenes and, alternating with these, representations of twelve priests and priestesses of Isis, each with his or her appropriate attributes and in the robes ordained for the ceremonial. Their faces and costumes are oriental, some of them unmistakably Semitic; the priests are beardless, have shaven heads, and are making hieratic gestures. Seven figures of this picture sequence have survived. Particularly striking is a boy priest with long, narrow feet, doubtless a novice, as his head is still unshaven. Wearing the ceremonial costume—white tunic and a long fringed cloak—and walking with measured steps, he carries with self-conscious dignity the ceremonial " situla of Isis " (a golden goblet) and a small pail containing the milk for the libation. With his lowered eyes and look of rapt absorption in his task, he reminds one of a child engaged on some grave, mysterious errand. The Pompeian painter has achieved a wonderfully lifelike rendering of a highly strung lad in the throes of adolescent mysticism; indeed, this figure is the most human, the nearest to us, of all the followers of the divine image in the Pompa Isidis.

THE THEATER

In few if any of the cities of the ancient world can enthusiasm for theatrical performances of all descriptions have run so high as in Pompeii. The most fashionable quarter of the city, in full view of the mountains and the sea, contained both a great open-air theater and the covered " Odeon," linked together by the long rows of porticos flanking the big *piazza*. There were any number of local mimes and actors, whose popularity is vouched for by the frequency with which we find their names incised on the walls in public places. Scenes from stage-plays often figure in the small pictures that have survived, while comic or tragic masks were freely used as motifs in interior decoration. Indeed one of the leading characteristics of much Pompeian wall-painting is its remarkable resemblance to stage scenery. Moreover, the subjects of many pictures are the same as those of the Greek and Roman drama, and it is obvious that the artists' more or less dramatic presentation of the adventures of the classical heroes and heroines (Hercules, Orestes, Phaedra, Medea, Iphigenia, for example) stemmed directly from plays they had seen performed on the stage. Some of the most attractive statuettes are terracotta effigies of characters in the farces known as *Atellanae Fabulae*, and no less noteworthy is a superb bronze portrait of the actor Norbanus Sorex, whose forthright modeling brings home to us so eloquently the emotive possibilities, convention not-withstanding, of the Roman actor's mask.

A taste for theatrical miming was innate in the Campanian populace, who responded instinctively to the give-and-take of histrionic dialogue and to the opportunities provided for the exteriorization of emotions by the use of mobile, strongly expressive masks. That stage performances, whether of the Greek or Roman type, were the delight not only of the populace but also of the well-to-do class (which was strongly imbued with Hellenistic fashions) is evident in the great number of paintings and mosaics dealing with such subjects. In the House of the Tragic Poet a small mosaic shows the preparations for a " satyr-drama "; an old actor is giving instructions to a group of young men dressed as satyrs, and in fact we feel we are seeing just what happened at a Roman rehearsal. A painting in the House of Quintus Poppaeus shows Menander unrolling the *volumen* of his comedies—a token of the high esteem in which the owner of this palatial mansion held the master of the Greek New Comedy. Lastly, we find, not only in the princely residence known as the House of the Centenary but also in a much humbler house in the area of the new excavations, little scenes from tragedies and comedies given the place of honor on the walls of the atrium—a further proof of the popularity of the contemporary stage with rich and poor alike.

But a survey of the paintings discovered at Pompeii and Herculaneum shows that this interest was not limited to scenes from plays; there was also much interest in theatrical personalities and we find likenesses of dramatists and individual actors. Of small dimensions and executed with remarkable *finesse*, these works resemble the " votive pictures " commissioned by competitors in musical or dramatic contests with a view to courting the favor of the gods. The chief figure is accompanied by various

THE PLAYER KING. FROM HERCULANEUM. MUSEO NAZIONALE, NAPLES.

secondary figures of an allegorical or theatrical order and in front of him are one or more masks, at which he gazes earnestly as at sacred emblems from which he hopes to draw timely inspiration.

One of the most attractive of these small pictures comes from Herculaneum, a city that also had its theater and seems to have been hardly less devoted than Pompeii to the stage. Painted in the purest neo-classical style, it formed part of a series of pictures stored for the time being in a room as yet undecorated, pending the day when it could be given its definitive place on the wall. A handsome, distinguished-looking young actor is seated on a stool. His hair is dishevelled, he has a high, finely modeled forehead and wears a long, almost sacerdotal chiton. The flowing whiteness of this garment, which emphasizes the nobility of his features, is interrupted only by a yellowish belt around the waist and the red cloak he has cast aside and let fall across his knees. With regal dignity he holds a scepter in his right hand, while with his left he grips the scabbard of his sword; posture, costume and attributes are those of the " player-king." Two neighboring figures reveal the meaning of this scene; on the "king's" left a young woman on her knees is writing a dedicatory inscription below a big tragic mask set up on a console, while another figure, presumably a minor actor, is watching or sponsoring the votive offering. Though the room in which the scene takes place is indicated only by a wall and a door through which light is entering from outside, and though no architectural elements are used for conveying the sense of space, this is adequately suggested by the slope given the console on which the mask is placed and by the relations of the various figures to this plane.

On the strength of certain similarities with busts and bas-reliefs said to depict Menander, the famous creator of the " New Comedy," some have thought that we have here his portrait. Against this is the fact that we should expect, were this Menander, to be shown a comic, not a tragic mask. Moreover, the most striking feature of this picture is its theatrical ambiance and elegant rendering of the traditional appearance of the player-king.

Of a livelier order and perhaps more congenial to the atmosphere of a Campanian town were scenes of Greek and Latin comedy, and the fact that versions of the scene we reproduce have been found both at Pompeii and at Herculaneum tends to show the great interest felt not only in the subject itself but also in the actors playing these comic roles. Here in fact we have one of the stock situations of Roman comedy: an interview between a courtesan and a servant, a parasite or a go-between—or, perhaps more likely, the surly " tutor " (guardian) of some rich young ne'er-do-well: a situation which was frequently used in the plays of Plautus and Terence, who took it over from Menander.

Wearing a huge, grimacing mask and with his legs planted far apart, the " tutor " cuts an ungainly figure; he is so squat and so fat that the cloak and tunic, though tightly wrapped around him, fail to hold in his bulging paunch. While casting a knowing glance at the public, he is making the familiar gesture of " the horns," intended to avert the evil eye. The younger of the two women is wearing a violet chiton and a richly decorated golden-yellow mantle. She has the thickly powdered face of the typical *hetaira*, and her black hair, clasped with a diadem, is dressed in a chignon in the Greek manner. Her parted lips, her hunched shoulders and air of concentrated fury give us the impression that she is hurling maledictions at the "tutor," who is trying, successfully we hope, to fend them off with the sign of the forked fingers. The other, more simply dressed woman, probably a maidservant, with her hand on her mistress's shoulder, seems to be trying to restrain her from coming to blows with the unwelcome visitor.

The fact that the same incident recurs, with only slight variants, in two works, one hailing from Pompeii, the other from Herculaneum, suggests that they had a common prototype, probably a work of high artistic quality, one of those small mural pictures of the neo-Attic school, a fine example of which figures later in this volume. None the less, such is the vivacity and freshness of the colors in the Pompeii picture that we may well imagine that the painter was working from the life and copying the vivid colors of a stage scene before him, or anyhow one with which he was familiar.

Hardly less in favor than subjects taken directly from the *pulpitum* (regular stage) and the ambiance of the theater were scenes from the country fairs, whose colorful exuberance was a characteristic feature of the squares and streets of the Hellenistic towns and seaports of Southern Italy. *The Street Musicians* is a small mosaic, one of two that figured in the so-called Villa of Cicero at Pompeii. It is signed in elegantly formed Greek characters, *Dioskourides of Samos*. This is thought to be the name of the mosaicist, who like the maker of the famous mosaic of *The Battle of Issus*, has here " translated " a painting into mosaic. The original model must certainly have enjoyed much renown both for the novelty of its subject and its artistic merits; this is confirmed by the fact that another copy (in point of fact rather a bad one) has been discovered at Stabiae. The mosaicist of Samos, on the other hand, indulged in a free and brilliant interpretation of the original. Hence the remarkable artistic quality of this little work which, though belonging to the long series of small genre scenes so dear to Hellenistic art, brings vividly before us one of the most picturesque and characteristic features of everyday life in the ancient world, seen through the eyes of an artist of distinction.

A troupe of strolling musicians is performing on the makeshift stage of a country fair; a stage which might equally well have served the turn of acrobats or jugglers. Its background is a yellow wall in which we see a house-door; presumably we are intended to visualize some Pompeian street and somewhere in the offing a little ring of interested onlookers. The troupe consists of four persons. Stocky, wrapped in garments so much too big for them that they have to hitch them up at the waist if they are to have any freedom of movement, these performers look more like Orientals than like Greeks; nor do the masks answer to the classical Greek type. One of them, the man facing us, is breaking into a dance step, holding a big tambourine that he is clapping with his right hand. He is singing, playing, dancing all at once, and we almost seem to hear the song, or, rather, street-ballad that is issuing from the comically twisted mouth. Another man, more heavily built and with coarser features—altogether a more vulgar type—is dancing to the sound of tiny cymbals he is clashing. Next we see a

THE COURTESAN. SCENE FROM A COMEDY. REGION I, INS. 6, NO. II, POMPEII.

THE STREET MUSICIANS. MOSAIC BY DIOSKOURIDES OF SAMOS. FROM THE VILLA OF CICERO, POMPEII.
MUSEO NAZIONALE, NAPLES.

meretriciously alluring woman (there is, one feels, something overdone in the sumptuousness of her garments and coiffure) playing the double pipes. Behind her a manikin with a wispy moustache seems to be waiting for his turn to join in the dance. This is obviously a street scene of an everyday order and there would be no point in trying to read any literary allusions or specific meaning into it. Nor should we be justified in assimilating these strolling musicians to the vagrant *soi-disant* votaries of Cybele (Metragyrtae), who performed during the intermissions at theaters. Rather, this little scene, taken straight from life, gives us a glimpse of what must have been a daily sight in the streets of a Roman town. Quite unpretentious, it has the raciness of an impromptu after-dinner speech made by some plebeian guest at Trimalchio's famous Banquet, as contrasted with the grave discourse of a statesman or an orator.

Nevertheless, the technique and style justify us in regarding this as one of the masterpieces of late Hellenic mosaic art. Its texture is extraordinarily minute and delicate, and, notably in the folds of garments, the tactile quality of rich tissues is beautifully rendered by subtle gradations of tints. The back wall, done in pinkish yellow, brings out the sheen of the red, white and brown mantles of the dancers; the yellow, blue and white of the dress of the woman playing the pipes. Indeed it is obvious that the artist has given much thought to his color effects, and we have here a foretaste of the almost impressionistic treatment of landscape and figures which came in during the age of Augustus.

PORTRAIT OF A LADY. MOSAIC FROM POMPEII. MUSEO NAZIONALE, NAPLES.

THE PORTRAIT

The Pompeian painters gave the faces and expressions of the gods, heroes, Satyrs and Bacchantes a quite startlingly human aspect, nor is it surprising that we owe to them a host of admirable portraits, in the form of medallions and small pictures. More or less idealized, many of these portraits came from the repertory of Greek iconography and depicted the philosophers, orators and poets in favor with the cultured Roman élite. But there were also family portraits and likenesses of contemporaries, which lack nothing of the plastic vigor of the world-famous works of sculpture discovered in Herculaneum and Pompeii. These pictures, however, are quite different from the commemorative statues or busts in bronze or marble which were set up in the Forum, in public buildings and in the *atria* of the residences of the nobility, and whose purpose was to glorify distinguished judges and public benefactors. The portraits we have now in mind served a sentimental purpose; they were intended to figure in private homes and to recall the features of the owner's loved ones, his wife or children. Sometimes, too, the likenesses of a married couple, who wished to bequeath to posterity a memorial of their life together, were painted on the walls.

Only one portrait in mosaic has been discovered in Pompeii and it is of quite outstanding interest. This mosaic was inset in the paved floor of a *cubiculum* and there can be little doubt of its being the portrait of some member of the household, most probably the *domina*, or lady of the house, whose cherished likeness was thus enshrined for ever in the privacy of the bedroom. It is executed in the finest, most delicate mosaic technique, the *opus vermiculatum*, and its close-grained texture resembles that of the small mosaic by Dioskourides of Samos. The artist's manipulation of the tesserae, so as to convey the subtlest nuances of color, and the skill with which he blends these are nothing short of masterly. A clean-cut line defines the head and shoulders, which stand out clearly on the uniform brown ground.

We have here the portrait of some high-born Pompeian lady; the features are distinctively Campanian. The cheeks are full, the lips rather thick, the flesh-tints natural, the neck somewhat massive and the sleek dark hair neatly parted in the middle. The expression of this lady's face is thoughtful, almost melancholy, and her bearing that of a dignified young housewife. Modeling is rendered by soft highlights on the flesh-tints, with zones of shadow on the periphery; indeed this mosaicist's handling of *sfumato* equals the most delicate effects obtainable by the painter's brush. The technique, however, is not impressionist. With its firmly knit composition this work reminds us of some of the Fayum portraits, and we can but regret that it is the sole example we possess of this highly accomplished art.

It is interesting to compare this lifelike, realistic portrait with the idealized, almost academically formal portrait of a young girl whose delicately molded features and tranquil gaze suggest that she belongs to a patrician *gens*. She has been " caught " by the painter in a meditative moment, when just about to record some thought or intimate emotion on the *tabellae* she is holding. Lightly resting the tip of her *stilus*

PORTRAIT OF A YOUNG GIRL. FROM POMPEII. MUSEO NAZIONALE, NAPLES.

PORTRAIT OF A WOMAN. FROM POMPEII. MUSEO NAZIONALE, NAPLES.

PORTRAIT OF A BAKER AND HIS WIFE. FROM POMPEII. MUSEO NAZIONALE, NAPLES.

on her lips, she has paused to reflect before continuing to write on the wax tablets clasped together like a book which she holds in her left hand. The carefully dressed curls framing the oval of her face and its dreamy expression bring to mind some 19th-century romantic portrait. We seem to have here a poetess in the throes of inspiration; indeed this was once believed to be a likeness of Sappho. In point of fact, however, this charming damsel with her refreshingly schoolgirlish air, whose *instrumentum scriptorium* is but a pretext for a high-romantic pose, is merely a well-bred young Pompeian, and the portrait might serve, at best, as a frontispiece for Ovid's *Heroides*.

The contrast between this portrait and the sensual, almost lascivious expression of the woman figuring in our next plate is striking. On the strength of the Phrygian cap and elegantly arranged curls some have thought that we here have Paris, the young shepherd from Mount Ida who ran away with Helen and judged the beauty contest between the goddesses. But though this possibility cannot be ruled out, it seems much more likely that this is the portrait of a woman no longer young, with a thick nose and rouged, fleshy lips, perhaps a well-known figure in Pompeian society. It is clear, anyhow, that the painter did not take his subject from the classical repertory, but drew inspiration from a real face, which he interpreted with warmly human understanding.

The Pompeian painters did not confine themselves to depicting fashionable ladies and elegant young girls. They also worked for a less cultured stratum: that of the *nouveau riche* craftsman, shopkeeper or business man, and it was largely owing to these contacts with members of the plebeian class, who expected a portrait to be a convincing likeness, that the Pompeian portrait-painter, too, developed that remarkable expressive power which characterizes the most famous statues of the ancient world.

An admirable illustration of this forceful realism is a picture, generally regarded as the masterwork of Pompeian portrait-painting, which was discovered on the wall of a *tablinum*. Since the house joined up with a bakery, it has now been decided, correctly in our opinion, that we here have likenesses of the baker and his wife and not, as the title originally given this famous picture led us to believe, those of P. Paquius Proculus and his wife. The man has a short straggly beard, coarse features, prominent cheek-bones: the face of a practical-minded peasant whose intelligence is limited to reckoning up his daily earnings. The woman, typically Campanian, looks crafty and perhaps something of a shrew, though there is a glint of coquetry in the large brown eyes. The fact that the man is holding a scroll and the woman an open writing tablet need not mislead us; these two people are too obviously unlettered, capable at best of entering up the accounts of their thriving bakery. In any case this affectation of literary interests was a foible of the Pompeians of the humbler ranks of society when sitting for their portraits—just as provincial couples pose for the photographer holding each other's hands. Here, the painter displays a skill and a sense of plastic values nowise inferior to those of the sculptor who made that famous portrait of the banker Lucius Caecilius Jucundus so revealing psychologically and so wonderfully " alive."

THE KNUCKLE-BONES PLAYERS. MONOCHROME ON MARBLE. FROM HERCULANEUM. MUSEO NAZIONALE, NAPLES.

THE GENRE SCENE

In addition to the classic myths, the theater and the human figure, painters, mosaicists, sculptors and workers in metal found a host of promising subjects ready to their hand in the life around them: aristocratic or plebeian themes, glimpses of home life and family meals, incidents in streets and markets, and their subjects ranged from highly idealized depictions of people and events to witty lampoons and the frankest eroticism. This variety of themes was paralleled by a diversity of styles and manners according as the artist was a neo-classic or a Campanian. Indeed, so copious is our material that we can do no more than draw attention to a few significant examples in the fields of painting and mosaic.

There have come down to us a small number of genre scenes by neo-Attic artists painted in the delicate encaustic technique on marble tablets. These have simple monochrome designs picked out with dainty touches of color and *sfumato*; indeed their exquisite linework and classic feeling for form recall the elegant refinement of Greek white-ground vase-painting. These were collectors' pieces, and though we have no sure record of the position of the tablets when discovered, it may be assumed that they were incrusted in the wall in prominent positions. Most of them were found at Herculaneum, and, whether or not they were actually produced there, their marketing center was, in all probability, Neapolis.

Their subjects are drawn from the repertory of classical art: Pirithous fighting the Centaur Eurytion, the grief of Niobe, the drunkenness of Silenus, chariot races, theatrical scenes. The most celebrated painting is that usually known as *The Knuckle-bones Players*, and inscribed " Alexander the Athenian painted this " ('Αλέξανδρος 'Αθηναῖος ἔγραφεν). The names of the five women are written on the picture: Leto, Niobe and Phoebe are standing, and squatting in front of them, intent on their game of knuckle-bones, are the two youngest of the group, Aglaia and Ileaira. Leto's attitude is one of cold reserve, and Phoebe seems to be urging Niobe to make a conciliatory move; here we can discern the effects (or a foretaste) of the bitter rivalry between the two mothers which led to the slaughter of Niobe's children. This charming scene of the two young girls playing their game with the gay lightheartedness of youth is certainly intended to emphasize the pathos of their impending fate. For behind the classic grace of this group of beautiful women we can sense conflicting emotions, the jealousy of the goddess and the protective instincts of the mother. We are probably indebted to an unknown neo-Attic artist for the remarkable purity of the composition in this small picture from Herculaneum, in which the lost beauty of some bas-relief of the age of Pheidias comes to life again.

We get interesting glimpses of Hellenistic life and customs in the small panels which, in the guise of painted tablets *(pinakes)*, figured in the upper tier of the best second- and third-style walls. They usually depicted interiors and scenes of family life (with an emphasis on the part played by women), or else scenes from the theater and the palaestra. As a matter of fact these subjects were quite unrepresentative of the

GYNAECEUM SCENE. TRICLINIUM OF THE IMPERIAL VILLA, POMPEII.

Roman way of life: a fact which goes to show how far the Roman élite went in their imitation of the customs, manners and fashions of the more refined Greek *milieu*. The very style of these delightful works, with their exquisitely finished execution, suggests the art of some neo-Attic painter or possibly a talented Campanian who made a point of scrupulously conforming to his neo-classical prototypes.

A charming sequence of these paintings can be seen on the walls of the large triclinium in the imperial villa recently brought to light near the Porta Marina at Pompeii, and we reproduce here two of the eight surviving pictures.

In one of them a young woman with finely molded features is seated in an alcove beside the *thalamus* (nuptial bed). Her veil, her sumptuous white robe and thoughtful look are those of a shy young wife. Beside her is a younger woman, gazing at her intently, and perhaps exchanging confidences. Beyond the alcove, at a window, stands a serving-maid, carrying a small perfume-jar or a *flabellum* shaped like an ivy-leaf; she seems to be waiting for a sign from her mistress to call to someone through the window. This is obviously a marriage scene, and recalls the *Aldobrandini Wedding* both in its setting and the arrangement and expression of the figures.

On the same frieze in the triclinium, alternating with scenes from the women's quarters, other panels represent games in the palaestra, obviously reminiscent of the Greek gymnasia for the athletic training of the *ephebi*. But, in any case, not only in the ancient Samnite palaestra of the theater district but also in the big palaestra of the Augustan age (near the Amphitheater), Pompeii had maintained in the institution of the " Juventus " the traditions and curriculum of the Attic *ephebia*. Thus it is not surprising to find in these small pictures the typical figures of an Hellenistic " gymnasium." A painting we reproduce depicts, in the classical three-figure lay-out, a scene of instruction in music and poetry. On the left, plucking the strings of an elegantly curved lyre which he is resting on a *podium*, stands a bearded man with a laurel-wreath on his head, his face aglow with inspiration; he wears the long coat affected by the pedagogues of the day. On the right is a comely woman whose head, unfortunately, has been badly damaged; clad in a sumptuous *himation* broadly draped across her body, she too is leaning against a high *podium*, holding in front of her an open papyrus-roll, lettered in Greek. In the center a boy, also wearing a wreath, intently follows the musician's every movement. Both these personages, especially the woman, may be regarded as allegorical personifications—of the arts of music and singing respectively. The boy, who is obviously taking a music lesson, has the same attentive attitude as the young Achilles of the painting in the Basilica of Herculaneum, where we see him being taught to play the cithara by the Centaur Chiron.

The composition of another panel, a " conversation piece " with three figures, is very similar. A dignified *matrona*, wearing a flowing white dress and a mantle of a darker hue, is sitting in a big chair with a rounded back, her feet resting on a stool —another proof of her exalted rank. Her eyes are fixed on a bearded old man, to whom she is listening attentively. Clad in a voluminous white mantle, his brows garlanded with leaves, he seems to be reading to her from the papyrus he is holding. Midway between him and the lady a little girl wearing a green sleeveless chiton stands listening with deferent attention. She holds some object like a basket with her left hand and in her right a little walking-stick. The scene is bathed in a tranquil bluish light flooding in from an open window in the background.

Alongside the output of stilted, artificial literature and art in the classic or classicizing manner, a very different kind of inspiration made its presence felt. For the Campanians were a naturally cheerful folk; they had a lively wit and keen sense of humor, which perhaps owed something to the comedies and mimes they flocked to see, with their somewhat risqué situations, their ribald jests and quick-fire dialogue,

THE MUSIC LESSON. TRICLINIUM OF THE IMPERIAL VILLA, POMPEII.

their practice of holding up to ridicule the *amours* of gods and heroes. Thus a new form of art arose, grotesque and caricatural, which, though some have traced its origin to the Alexandrian *grylloi*, found what was certainly its raciest expression in Campanian painting.

Olympus itself was the first target of the artists' ridicule. A frieze (unfortunately in a bad state of preservation) from the bathroom in the House of Menander depicts in mock-heroic style some episodes in the lives of the gods—but gods no taller than dwarfs, with grotesquely big heads and puppet-like gestures. One shows a tousle-haired Jupiter at his wits' end, what with the jealous vigilance of Juno, the spying eyes of Isis, and the aggressiveness of Venus who, in the guise of a vindictive shrew, is egging Cupid on to turn his arrows against the ruler of the gods. In another picture

TEACHER AND PUPIL. TRICLINIUM OF THE IMPERIAL VILLA, POMPEII.

we see Minerva, with a huge helmet cupping her plump moon-face, arching her brows in the best comic manner as she watches the musical contest between Apollo and Marsyas which was to end so disastrously for the latter.

With Virgil's *Aeneid* then at the height of its popularity, it was only to be expected that Aeneas should come in for some rough handling by the comedians and painters. Thus we find a small picture showing Aeneas, travestied as a big bear, in flight from Troy with old Anchises perched like a fat monkey on his shoulders and little Ascanius, who has the muzzle of a bear-cub, vainly trying to keep pace with the huge strides of his father. This burlesque of the Aeneid not only testifies to the great vogue of the Aeneas legend, but also to the irrepressible wit of a race that dared so lightheartedly to mock the eminent progenitor of the *Gens Julia*.

THE JUDGMENT OF SOLOMON. DETAIL. FROM POMPEII. MUSEO NAZIONALE, NAPLES.

THE PYGMIES' HUNT, DETAIL. FROM POMPEII. MUSEO NAZIONALE, NAPLES.

"CAVE CANEM." MOSAIC FROM POMPEII. MUSEO NAZIONALE, NAPLES.

SILENUS AND HIS ASS. MOSAIC FROM THE HOUSE OF PAQUIUS PROCULUS, POMPEII. MUSEO NAZIONALE, NAPLES.

A Biblical theme is amusingly parodied in a Pompeian painting of *The Judgment of Solomon*. The scene is laid in a praetorium, and the artist has deliberately emphasized the bleakness of the court-room so as to show up to best effect the ungainly attitudes of the dwarfish, topheavy figures. The action is divided between three groups: the bearded judges in white togas, gravely seated on the *suggestum*; soldiers in shadow behind them, and behind the raised platform of the court more soldiers, with glittering helmets and breast-plates, drawn up in line. In the center the tiny body of the child lies ready for bisection by the executioner's knife, while the two claimants stand by, the true mother reduced to such utter despair that she seems a mere bundle of quivering rags. Slightly to one side are grouped the horrified spectators, torn between curiosity and dismay.

The Egyptian landscape of the Upper Nile with its pygmies and queer beasts was a godsend for the caricaturist painters, who made great play with the comic effects produced by the contrast between the Lilliputian stature and misshapen bodies of the hunters, with their spindle legs and monstrous heads, and the terrifying bulk of the wild animals they have to contend with. Across a broad expanse of river, with houses, trees, jetties and boats glimmering in a pale, misty light, we see the pygmies performing grotesque feats of valor as they hunt down crocodiles and hippopotami. One is sitting proudly astride the crocodile that his friends are dragging forward, while another digs a spear into the rump of a hippopotamus which meanwhile is placidly chewing up a luckless dwarf. Another, greatly daring, is pummeling with his fists a crocodile armed with a fearsome array of teeth. This fabulous land beyond the sea, peopled with strange monsters and tiny men, had a great appeal to artists and writers and it continued to figure, with little change, in legends of later times, notably in the mediaeval tales of chivalry.

Sketches and genre scenes of this lively, popular order were often executed in mosaic, and these works were not only in the style of the sophisticated neo-Attic art (as seen in the *Street Musicians* by Dioskourides of Samos), but also of a purely local kind. These latter were turned out in large numbers by artisans and guilds, perhaps resident in Pompeii and certainly of Campanian origin.

The *Cave canem* theme of the watchdog chained up on the threshold *(canis catenarius)* attracted much attention on its discovery at Pompeii in the form of a mosaic figuring in the floor of the House of the Tragic Poet. More recently a similar mosaic has been found in the House of Paquius Proculus, and there is yet a third version, little known to the public and also originating from Pompeii, which can be seen in the Naples Museum. This is a relatively small work executed in rather large tesserae —which suggests that it figured in some modest home. In it the artist has achieved amazing expressive power with great economy of means.

Held back by a leash fastened to his collar, the dog is baring his fangs. He is placed diagonally across the square of the mosaic with his forelegs stretched out in front and his hind legs splayed out. His reddish eyes are dilated, his claws are out, his ears pricked up and his jaws agape—in fact we feel he would like nothing better than to

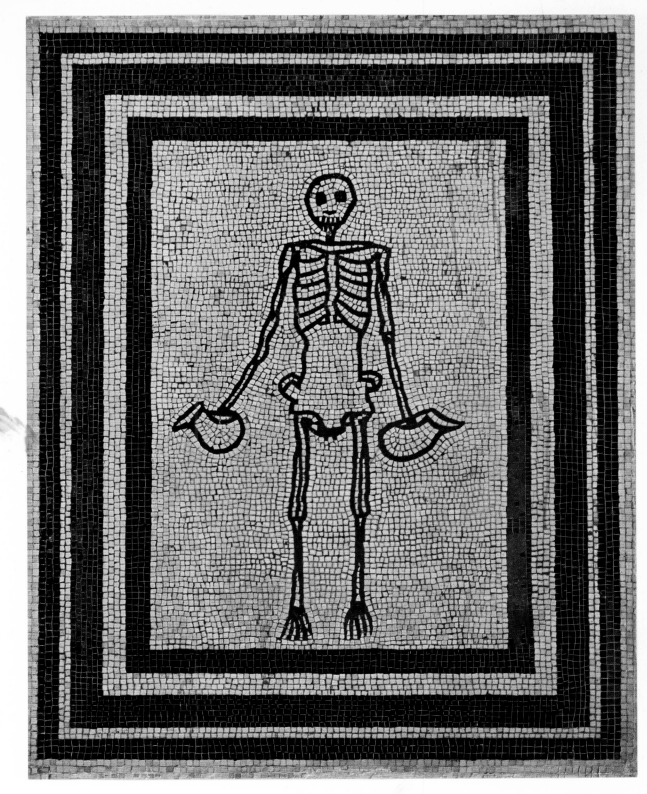

SKELETON OF A BUTLER. MOSAIC FROM POMPEII. MUSEO NAZIONALE, NAPLES.

sink his teeth in the leg of some unwary visitor. Though an almost uniform black mass, the body is given mobility and vitality by the rim of white cubes following its curves and stressing its plastic values. The only breaks in this uniform blackness are red and white specks on the collar, the lolling tongue, the eye, the ears and claws —and these small but effective touches of color admirably convey the impression aimed at, that of a watchdog valiantly defending his master's threshold.

A similar technique is employed in the picture of Silenus and his ass, which, with its healthy, unforced humor, might well be the replica of some comic scene with Satyrs depicted on an Attic vase. Of quite small dimensions (22 ¾" × 22 ¼"), it originally formed part of the floor in the stately House of Paquius Proculus. We see a fat old Silenus, obviously the worse for drink, sliding off the back of his mount, an unfortunate ass which has collapsed under the weight of its rider. Two young men, dressed more like townsfolk than the Satyrs we should expect to figure in a picture of this kind, are trying to lift the animal on to its feet, by tugging at its ears and tail. (This amusing little scene might figure as an illustration to Franco Sacchetti's entertaining story of the ass that lost its tail.)

The mosaicist has used rather large cubes, irregularly arranged in imitation of the *vermiculatum* technique. The figures stand out sharply from the shadowless background, and colors are handled in the impressionist manner, building up light effects without tonal transitions. The flesh of Silenus and his rescuers is reddish and the animal's body uniformly black; the harness is pale yellow and the men's garments are light brown. Essential details of the faces are briefly indicated by cubes of various colors. Such is the organic unity of the composition and the balanced distribution of the masses that our Pompeian artist may well have followed some prototype—possibly a mosaic—of classical antiquity. Be this as it may, he certainly had a keen sense of humor and indulged it here to the happiest effect.

Alongside these cheerful scenes, the effigy of Death often makes an appearance on the walls and floors of houses, perhaps in pursuance of the Epicurean theory that a good way of forgetting life's vexations when at table is to have a grim reminder of death before our eyes. Amongst the gruesome emblems that figured in the triclinium (e.g. ghosts of defunct guests, the skulls in the Boscoreale treasure) none is more effective than this skeleton of a butler done in mosaic on the floor of a triclinium. Framed within three plain black bands the skeleton, black too, tells out strongly against the white cubes of the background, holding a wine-jug in each hand. Noticeable here, too, are the Pompeian artist's skillful distribution of the picture surface and the fine economy of his draftsmanship. And we are reminded of the lines Trimalchio recited to his guests after exhibiting to them the *larva convivialis* (in modern parlance, " the skeleton at the feast "):

> *Sic erimus cuncti, postquam nos ceperit Orcus.*
> *Ergo vivamus, dum licet esse, bene.*

Not great poetry perhaps, but rich in ancient wisdom...

5

NATURE IN POMPEIAN PAINTING
LANDSCAPE

Landscape was given a large place in Campanian art, and there can be no doubt that owners of houses liked seeing views of the Campanian countryside with its graceful hills and vistas opening on the sea depicted on their walls, and that the artists, too, enjoyed painting these subjects. Whether or not the Romans were pioneers in the field, it is certain that they had much fondness for country life. What poet has shown a truer feeling for nature than we find in Virgil ? Noteworthy, too, was the Romans' habit of building their country houses in groves, on wooded hillsides, and in places with sea views. This Roman love of nature is confirmed not only by the tradition that an Italian artist named Studius or Ludius was the inventor (or renovator) of landscape-painting, but also by the great number of landscapes figuring on the walls of houses, large and small alike, in the three Campanian towns. Sometimes an entire wall is painted so as to give the illusion of a garden; elsewhere landscape friezes run all round a room; and, again, there are small, isolated pictures giving as it were glimpses of the out-of-doors across the walls, and thus " opening " the walls even more effectively than any architectural vista.

From the Second Style onwards, landscape bulked large in the paintings with mythological or epic subjects. It took a poetic, idealized form in scenes of the wanderings of Ulysses, while the themes of *Perseus and Andromeda, Daedalus and Icarus, Polyphemus and Galatea* were set in seascapes, with beetling cliffs. When extending over an entire frieze or panel, it became the leading theme, the mythological figures being relegated to a secondary role. In these cases the landscape is pastoral or idyllic, painted in what looks like a naïve, spontaneous manner, but often with a studied elegance, and the painters tend to use such familiar, not to say hackneyed, motifs as little rustic shrines sheltering under big, leafy trees with domestic animals grazing all around, and wayfarers contemplating the holy place in attitudes of humble reverence. Indeed, the architectural features—whether sanctuaries, small temples, chapels, hamlets, country houses, harbors, jetties or swimming-pools—are often treated as the leading theme and dominate the entire composition.

It should, however, be noted that these architectural elements were not so much in the Campanian style as in that of Graeco-Roman Egypt, or the hellenizing art of the islands and coasts of Asia Minor. In any case (except in some works where landscape proper is the leading theme) the painter did not set out to paint the " likeness " of any real place; he built up an imaginary world, into which, however, he inserted fragments of remembered scenes. In all these paintings the color is subdued, romantic, and there is a poetic glamour, a delicately naïve charm, that still has its appeal.

CUPID PUNISHED. FROM THE HOUSE OF "CUPID PUNISHED," POMPEII. MUSEO NAZIONALE, NAPLES.

PAN MAKING MUSIC WITH THE NYMPHS. FROM POMPEII. MUSEO NAZIONALE, NAPLES.

After the first appearance of the impressionistic landscape in the big " yellow frieze " of the House of Livia (in company with classical architectural and figure themes), landscape came to be handled in a rapid, sketchy technique, all in nuances of light and shade, with only the briefest indications of the essentials of form, color and movement. This method of painting (which the Roman writers named *ars compendiaria*) had something in common with the illusionist procedures of modern Impressionism. Contours dissolve into the surrounding air; objects and bodies are suggested by simple tonal relations, the interplay of light and shadow. The figures in these landscapes (especially the late fourth-style landscapes) are hinted at by a few dabs of color or sudden gleams of light, as if momentarily glimpsed in the act of movement. Such is the violence of these clashes of light and shade in certain pictures, that the landscape itself ceases to be static. In these strange pictures devoid of atmosphere and painted on monochrome grounds, red, green, yellow, black or blue (but not the blue of air), where only the intensity of tones furnishes the indispensable relief, forms are disintegrated, almost to the point of obliteration. Here we have nothing short of a technical revolution, indicative of the wholly new approach of the Roman painter to his art. Seen against the light, in a quivering haze of broken gleams, the landscape seems the fabric of a dream that would promptly vanish like an " unsubstantial pageant " were the play of light and shade to cease. Sometimes, too, a sort of breeze seems to be faintly ruffling the surface of the colors, and then we are reminded of those aerial Chinese landscapes painted on silk, and of the ceramics of the East.

In Pompeian painting the earliest type of landscape art (obviously stemming from the Hellenistic bas-reliefs) can be seen in a group of pictures seemingly the work, if not of the same master, of the same atelier. These are mythological or genre scenes in the purest neo-classical style and the settings consist of rocks and trees, whose color gradations indicate the various planes. An example is *Cupid Punished*, in which a tiny Eros, escorted by one of the Graces, is whimpering because Aphrodite, who is gazing at him sadly and severely, has confiscated his quiver. The setting of this charming little scene (perhaps a pictorial version of some neatly turned Alexandrian epigram) is not, as one would have expected, a garden or Aphrodite's palace, but a definitely Hellenistic landscape. The scene is divided into two parts by a leafy tree, while the background consists of rocks and barren trees. The harmony between the incident depicted and its setting is even more complete in another small, delightful picture of *Pan making Music with the Nymphs*. A slim young man seated on a rock, Pan is waiting till the cithara-player has finished her prelude before starting to play on his pipes. The scene is bathed in a luminous calm, as if it too were held spellbound by the entrancing melody.

These landscapes are definitely classical in conception; both design and colors are tranquil and harmonious, and they serve chiefly as a framework for the mythological or poetic scenes depicted. But when we come to our two next pictures (selected from a host of similar works), illustrating the last, impressionist manner of fourth-style

HOUSES AT NOON. FROM POMPEII. MUSEO NAZIONALE, NAPLES.

Pompeian painting, we cannot fail to see that a drastic change has come over Pompeian art, no less as regards its choice of subjects than as to its handling of color. In one of these panels the main subject is a group of buildings in the countryside: a shed, a shrine (or a well), a low, square farmhouse with long rows of windows. Such few figures as there are stand in the foreground and are sketchily indicated by patches of light and shade. Shafts of vivid light play on the houses and figures, while the patches of shadow within the houses and on the human forms seen against the light stand out as clots of vibrant darkness, while the background is a vague expanse of greenish grey. Indeed the whole scene is bathed in an eerie, almost other-worldly atmosphere.

Another picture we reproduce, though it keeps to the normal procedure of the sacred-idyllic landscape, has a poetic beauty and an emotive quality all its own. Spatial recession is suggested by a dextrous handling of light and perspective. We see a hallowed precinct, perhaps a sacred island, surrounded by a sort of moat spanned by a one-arched bridge. Two spiky crags loom up in the background; in front of them are clumps of trees and a row of tapering cypresses. That this is holy ground is evident from the nature of the buildings. In the center is a *tetrapylon* for the worship of a sacred tree; near by are two small temples, altars, another shrine and, well in the foreground, a statue, perhaps of Diana Lucifera, the Light-bringer. Some cows can be seen slowly moving across the water on the right, while the shepherd, followed by a goat, who is

SACRED LANDSCAPE. FROM POMPEII. MUSEO NAZIONALE, NAPLES.

crossing the bridge adds a pastoral accent to the scene. All is suffused in the vivid green light emanating from the sky and water, across which rise, dappled with rust-red glints, the cliffs and temples.

Particularly interesting are the views of real scenes, and it is regrettable that there are so few of them. One is a harbor scene showing a pier, a lighthouse, wharves, a triumphal arch, commemorative pillars, fishing-boats and stately ships. Around the harbor are temples, arcades and dwelling houses with loggias and terraces. Some have seen in this a picture of the harbor of Pozzuoli; but, besides the fact that it was found in the old town of Stabiae, there are better grounds for thinking it represents one of the many Campanian ports. Be this as it may, we have in this small picture one of the most striking impressionist creations of Campanian art. A light breeze is playing on the blue expanse of land-locked water, making it glitter in the sun, while the darker masses of jetties, wharves and the lighthouse are faceted with golden glints, that gradually lose their brilliance in aerial perspective. If we disregard the arcades and columns, this might well pass for a 19th-century Neapolitan seascape, and indeed the handling of light and color is not unlike that of such painters as Giacinto Gigante.

HARBOR SCENE. FROM STABIAE. MUSEO NAZIONALE, NAPLES.

TREE WITH SNAKE. NEW EXCAVATIONS, REGION I, INS. 9, NO. 5, POMPEII.

HERON IN A GARDEN. NEW EXCAVATIONS, REGION II, INS. 6, NO. 3, POMPEII.

GARDENS AND ANIMALS

Of no less interest are the garden scenes which, painted on the walls of peristyles and real gardens, gave the illusion of prolonging the natural vista of shrubs and clumps of flowers into a vast green park depicted on the wall. Sometimes, too, the wall space of a room was painted so as to produce the impression of opening out upon fields or wooded hillsides. For the Roman city-dweller took a real pleasure in having before his eyes reminders of the amenities of a country house. The ultimate origin of this practice may be the *hortus* which in the remote past formed an integral part of the Roman home and kept the household supplied with vegetables. In the course of time the *hortus* developed into the *viridarium*, a garden with shrubs and flowers symmetrically laid out, and adorned with fountains, nymphaea and statuary. In these *viridaria* art

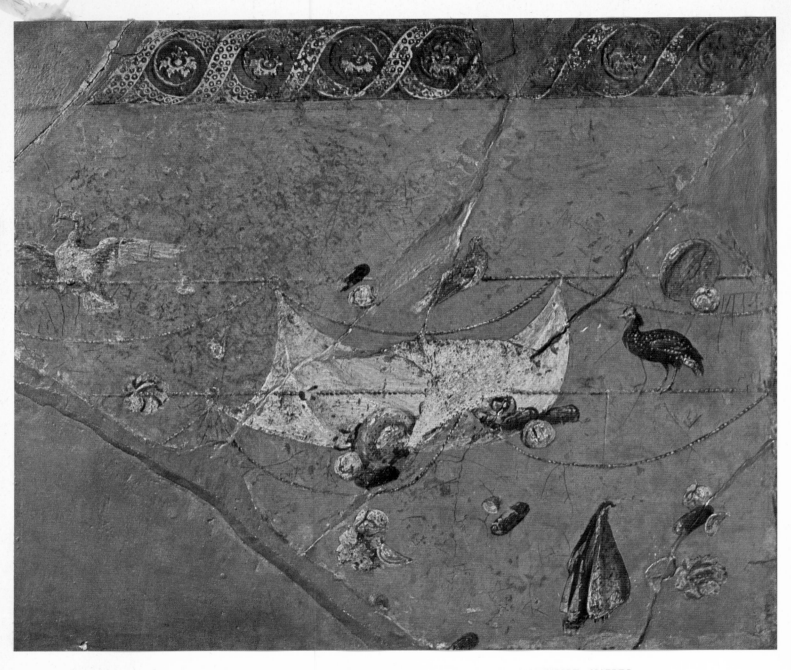

BIRDS, FLOWERS AND FRUIT. FROM POMPEII. MUSEO NAZIONALE, NAPLES.

and nature joined forces to the happiest effect; they were indeed the ancestors of the parks and formal gardens which in later days were the pride of many an Italian country house. Naturally enough the painters took notice of the new taste for so-called " landscape gardening," the style of painting representing these being described as *opus topiarium*. Happily, in contrast to this art which became more and more devitalized, some painters made views of landscapes in which the trees, instead of being geometrically arrayed and looking like illustrations in a manual of botany, were treated in a more imaginative way. The most elaborate composition of this order was discovered in the Villa of Livia at Prima Porta, but similar decorations existed in many Pompeian houses and villas. We find them in the *cubiculum* of the Villa Boscoreale, in the House of Diomedes, in the garden of the House of Sallust and in the House of Orpheus; also in the courtyards and gardens of smaller houses, and, lastly, in the *frigidarium* of the Thermae at Stabiae where those who used the swimming-pool had the impression of being in a little lake surrounded by greenery.

While fruit often appears in the still life, orchards figure comparatively rarely in Pompeian landscape art. Two such pictures have, however, been discovered in the course of recent excavations at Pompeii, in *cubicula*. The fruit-trees—cherry-trees, fig-trees, plum-trees, pear-trees, service-trees, arbutus and a few lemon-trees— indicate the various kinds of fruit grown at Pompeii (or, rather, in the *horti Pompeiani*). It was an orchard of this kind that Trimalchio, with *nouveau riche* affectation, disdained

BIRDS. NEW EXCAVATIONS, REGION I, INS. 9, NO. 5, POMPEII.

TURTLEDOVES. MOSAIC FROM THE HOUSE OF THE FAUN, POMPEII. MUSEO NAZIONALE, NAPLES.

to recognize as his, but which his steward did not fail to mention in his reports *(Cena Trimalchionis, LIII)*. On the glossy black wall of a *cubiculum* is depicted a fig-tree laden with ripe fruit and a serpent winding its way up the trunk towards a bird's nest hidden in the foliage. On another wall we see arbutus-trees, sprinkled with red, rough-coated berries, interspersed among flowering bay-trees, and the painter has depicted these with the loving care of a naturalist, rendering each detail with meticulous precision: the exact shape and veins of the leaves, the soft curves of young branches, the various shades of green on the same tree, the differences between the stems of the leaves and those of the fruit. This holds good even when the artist permits himself a certain stylization, as in the case of a fig-tree, whose trunk is over-smooth and over-slender and all of whose lobate leaves are open and turning the same way, while all the figs are equally ripe. This is an exceptional case, however, and does not alter the fact that nature pure and simple was one of the chief sources of inspiration of Roman decorative art from the Augustan age onward.

HERON AND SNAKE. FROM POMPEII. MUSEO NAZIONALE, NAPLES.

Almost always in the garden and orchard scenes birds play a leading part and, whether common or exotic, are delineated with a liveliness and a realism that say much for the artist's keenness of eye and his interest in natural life. We can see that he has closely studied the habits and even the methods of flight of many kinds of birds; black and white turtledoves, magpies, swallows and blackbirds in flight or perched on branches, on the edges of vases, or on an entablature, and with their flutterings to and fro they add a touch of animation to the immobility of shrubs and fruit-trees. We know that aviaries and dove-cotes were in high favor with the Pompeians; thus it is not surprising that birds, turtledoves especially, appear so often in their paintings and mosaics. The classical prototype of the famous picture of doves perched on the edge of a marble bowl of water, from which they are drinking, is attributed to Sosos of Pergamum. In the little scene of this order which we reproduce, the work of a Pompeian mosaicist, the composition is remarkably free, with a color-scheme in which black and white predominate. Here only essential colors are employed, and the linework, too, is reduced to essentials; thus this little scene strikes a contrast with the elaborate polychrome mosaics composed of myriads of multicolored cubes.

The white forms of the three doves stand out sharply against the black ground; their wings, eyes and beaks are briefly indicated by specks of black or red. One of the birds has been delving in an old-fashioned jewel-box with red and yellow sides and fished up a bead necklace, some of the beads of which have slipped off and are falling to the ground. The two other doves are clinging to the side of the box, one of them pecking at the necklace.

We must not forget that though the Pompeian painter sometimes observed nature with the eye of a naturalist, this never inhibited his instinct for decorative effect. From amongst the countless compositions on subjects drawn from the animal or vegetable kingdom, we have selected one of a remarkable and somewhat intriguing order. The ground color is cobalt blue, its top margin being defined by a frieze resembling a ribbon. In the center is a sort of hammock hung high in air and birds, depicted with the precision of a miniaturist, are perching on the ropes. Fruit, flowers and other more or less indeterminate objects seem to be floating down from the upper air. Are we to see these as the flowers and gifts that a hospitable host sometimes let fall on his guests through an opening in the ceiling? But there is little point in looking for an " explanation " of this curious picture; we do better simply to admire the artist's fine decorative sense and the aerial fluidity of this art, which a modern critic might well describe as " metaphysical."

The provinces oversea, Egypt especially, had familiarized the Romans with a motley assortment of exotic animals. The big Praeneste mosaic, another in the House of the Faun, and the numerous decorations with Egyptian settings found in Pompeii show the attraction that the animal life of the banks of the Nile and the fabulous land of the Pygmies had for the artists. And they were not content with depicting domestic or exotic animals in repose, as if posing for their pictures, but often tried to show them in the act of fighting. Thus one famous mosaic gives a realistic represen-

tation of a cockfight. A less known but highly effective picture shows a fight between a heron and a ureus (cobra). They are confronting each other before starting the last round, and the heron, whose silvery plumage still bristles with the fury of the first encounter, is aiming his long, sharp beak at the snake's head. Shored up on its viscous coils, with its hood expanded, the snake is craning its neck forward, about to strike at the heron with its venomous fangs.

THE SACRED BULL. FROM THE TEMPLE OF ISIS, POMPEII. MUSEO NAZIONALE, NAPLES.

The sanguinary " games " that took place in the amphitheater gave the Romans plenty of opportunities of studying the habits and appearance of wild beasts. Amongst the decorations on the walls of peristyles and gardens we sometimes have scenes of big-game hunting in Africa, on the banks of the Nile or in Asia (then little known). Lions, panthers, hippopotami, elephants and wild bulls (bull-fights were as popular with the Romans as with the Spaniards) were shown in suitably " wild " settings of rocks and spiky, leafless trees.

Sometimes the subject derives from iconography, as in the painting of the sacred bull Apis which figured in the Temple of Isis at Pompeii. Its massive bulk is solidly poised on short, thick legs, and the bony structure underlying the uniform, flat color of the body is skillfully suggested. This stately, ponderous figure brings to mind a basalt statue in some ancient temple.

THE STILL LIFE

Though today we tend to regard the still life as essentially an achievement of Flemish, French and Italian art, it had already a conspicuous place in ancient mural painting, or, more precisely, in that of Campania. For, with very few exceptions, all the ancient still lifes extant figured in decorations discovered at Pompeii, Herculaneum and Stabiae during the excavations begun in the 18th century and still in progress.

Roman and Campanian painters cannot, however, claim to be the originators of the still life, for some Greek artists of the Hellenistic period, both painters and mosaicists, had already made a name for themselves by painting small objects, food and drink, and even scraps fallen from the table. We know of these works only from descriptions of them given by ancient writers. Thus Pliny tells us of the mosaicist Sosos whose picture of the " Unswept Floor " of a dining-room created quite a sensation in its day. It may have been this work which gave rise to an ancient pun. Instead of using the term " rhopography " (i.e. depiction of odds and ends) to describe this kind of painting whose subject-matter was the scraps of food lying on a dining-room floor, the Greeks mockingly baptized it " rhyparography " (i.e. painting of the sordid). Actually, though they regarded it as a minor art, the ancients appreciated the still life no less than we do today. Indeed, if Pliny is to be trusted *(N. H. XXXV, 112)* the most popular *rhyparographos* of the day, one Piraeicus, who painted pictures of foodstuffs, animals and interiors of humble barbers' and bootmakers' shops, succeeded in selling his small pictures at higher prices than those commanded by the most eminent contemporary painters.

Artists at Herculaneum and Pompeii catered to the taste for the still life, and so rich and varied was their handling of it that we have here one of the most interesting aspects of all ancient mural painting. Such themes, moreover, were in keeping with the spirit of an age when the pleasures of the table lay not in good food alone, but also in handsome silver dinner services, fine glass and terracotta ware, and in the custom of making presents *(xenia)* to guests at dinner-parties. And this practice obtained at all social levels, from Horace's frugal table to the lavish banquets of Trimalchio.

A favorite subject of the Pompeian still life was the produce of the rich Campanian vineyards and orchards, and the fish and game served up at table. All sorts of fruit were depicted: fresh, dried and stuffed figs, peaches, plums, raisins, green and purple grapes, and even fruit that had only recently been acclimatized in Campania, such as cherries, or was imported from oversea, like dates and pineapples. The game, however, was always native to the region: hares, thrushes and partridges, which were trapped in snares in the region between Vesuvius and the Monti Lattari. The bays and rivers supplied the painter and mosaicist with a great variety of subjects : shell-fish, cuttle-fish, tiny silvery fish leaping out of the fisherman's creel, huge skates hung like trophies on the red background of the wall. Nor did the artists disdain such dairy products as cheeses tied in plaited reeds and poultry raised in the farmyards of the country houses.

BOWLS OF FRUIT AND AMPHORA. FROM THE HOUSE OF JULIA FELIX, POMPEII. MUSEO NAZIONALE, NAPLES.

Naturally enough, the still life underwent the same progressive changes as mural painting in general. Realistic in second-style painting, its vigorous, colorful forms are seen to much effect in the large-scale compositions of the Villa Boscoreale, the Villa of Julia Felix and the House of the Cryptoporticus. When the Third Style brought in an art as meticulous and dainty as miniature-painting, the still life followed suit and was fined down to stylized, decorative renderings of birds and flowers. The Fourth Style, however, brought back the taste for a wealth and variety of naturalistic motifs. But though the themes remained the same (fruit, game, fish, and all that goes to make a sumptuous repast), the conception of the picture changed completely. The impressionist way of seeing which had so brilliantly come into its own in landscape-painting now prevailed in the composition and color effects of the still life. Yet, despite its popularity, it was never given a central place in mural decorations—not even in the Pompeii meat market *(Macellum)* where, for obvious reasons, one would have expected it to figure prominently. It was always relegated to a subordinate place: as a frieze, for example, divided into panels that spaced out the various objects and articles of food represented, or in vignettes painted on each side of a central panel; sometimes, too, it figured in isolated scenes which, though devoid of any real compositional scheme, charm the eye with their fresh, gay colors.

The Pompeian artists painted fruit, game and fish with such spontaneous, almost sensual gusto that we are tempted to compare them with certain Neapolitan painters of the 17th and 18th centuries. They drew inspiration not only from well-appointed tables, laden with crystal goblets and silverware, but also from the everyday sights of the market-place in the Forum. We can picture them feasting their eyes on a fresh catch of fish glittering in the sun, or lingering over the baskets of grapes and peaches glowing so appetizingly, then as now, in the open-air markets of Naples. For the Pompeian artist was a born observer; he had the keen eye of a peasant, for whom nature has no secrets. Moreover, he had an instinctive understanding of animals, and painted them in their most natural attitudes, not without an occasional touch of humor: a rabbit, whose greediness has got the better of his fear, munching a bunch of ripe grapes; a bird pecking at a cherry or a juicy fig; a cock haughtily stalking away from a basket whose contents, however, he is itching to sample.

STILL LIFE WITH EGGS AND GAME. FROM THE HOUSE OF JULIA FELIX, POMPEII. MUSEO NAZIONALE, NAPLES.

PEACHES AND GLASS JAR. FROM HERCULANEUM. MUSEO NAZIONALE, NAPLES.

Here in fact we have a racy handling of everyday subjects somewhat akin (as pointed out above) to that of Seicento and Settecento art. Nevertheless, the engaging simplicity and mellowness of tones, combined with boldness in the rendering of vibrant light and color and, above all, the unusual lay-out of these compositions, have more in common with certain present-day trends in painting. For while the 17th- and 18th-century Neapolitan painters cluttered up the canvas with all the gifts of Nature in an orgy of colors and forms that flatter the eye but mean little to us, the Campanian artist restricted himself to a few isolated objects carefully arranged. Not that he had any bias towards " metaphysical " painting; it was rather that he aimed at a highly concentrated art synthesizing his poetic response to visual experience. For, despite his seeming naturalism, he too saw the world through the eyes of a poet and sought to transfigure it accordingly.

Indeed the Pompeian painter's arrangement of a still life was remarkably like that of our present-day artists. Fruit, game and fish are laid out on one or two plain wooden surfaces, either the benches on which the food was placed in the *triclinia*, or the well-stocked shelves of a cupboard. But this was no more than a starting-off point; for the Roman artist was quite as well aware as any modern that he must hold the observer's interest by a skillful disposition of planes combined with a respect for natural appearances, by judicious touches of color and passages of vibrant light, so as to enliven the almost neutral tones of shell-fish, mollusks and fowl made ready for the kitchen.

The first outstanding still lifes we possess—obviously belonging to the Second Style—come from the Praedia Juliae Felicis, a country house on the outskirts of the town, first discovered in 1755-1757, then neglected and rediscovered only last year. The spacious grounds around the house may very well have included an extensive fruit-garden—which would account for the presence of paintings of this order, some of which probably figured in the nymphaeum in the garden, used as an out-door dining-room.

In our first still life the objects are arranged on two levels, most prominent being a big crystal bowl containing fruit of various kinds. So apt is the coloring and so unctuous the modeling that one senses their succulent ripeness, particularly effective being the bunch of small, purplish grapes still attached to an already dried-up stem. An apple has fallen out of the bowl, also a pomegranate which has split in falling, letting some of its seeds escape. On the lower tier we see an earthenware jar containing grapes, against which is propped a small closed amphora, the lid held down by a length of string looped round its ears. One wonders what is in it: olives, raisins, honey or some other delicacy relished by its owner ? Here we have none of the impressionist effects characteristic of the Fourth Style. Each fruit, every grape, no less than the form and color of the three vases, is rendered with the painstaking care and attention to detail which we associate with the Flemings rather than with the painter of antiquity.

Our next picture also comes from the House of Julia Felix, where it figured with three other panels (in a poorer state of preservation) in a frieze extending the full length of a wall. The objects are set out on a rectangular cube whose form is indicated with geometrical precision. Volumes are skillfully balanced, on the extreme left being a bronze vessel across which lies a ladle, in the center a dish of large eggs, and on the right an *oinochoe* in burnished metal, with a three-lobed mouth and a handle daintily edged in white. On the wall just above the eggs four thrushes, hung by their beaks, form a symmetrical group. Leaning against the socle is a small white, cylindrical amphora with a seal on its mouth and bearing an inscription—which, however, records neither its contents nor the painter's name. Above it a fringed napkin or duster hangs on the wall. There is an almost mathematical symmetry in the way the various objects are disposed: the eggs and game in the center, and on either side the burnished vessels. Highlights splashed on the necks and bodies of the latter and on the smooth surface of the eggs, together with the more intricate light-effects on the plumage of the birds, bring out their plastic values, while the napkin, drooping in graceful folds, adds a note of elegance to the relative austerity of the *ensemble*.

The composition is freer and the naturalistic effect more pronounced in our next still life: of two shelves in a larder on which we see the branch of a peach-tree with the fruit attached, and a glass jar. The former is not so much resting on the shelf as hung across the foreground in such a way as to emphasize the smoothly flowing curves of the branch and the young leaves. One of the peaches has been detached from the branch and a small piece cut out of it, showing the pale, unripe flesh. The glass jar, half filled with water, has an exquisite translucence, dappled here and there with silvery glints. Like others of the Fourth Pompeian Style, this picture shows that the painter had made great strides in the understanding of nature and, by the same token, of naturalistic illusionism. Yet such terms as " naturalism " and " illusionism " do not suffice to explain the peculiar charm of these still lifes; perhaps its origin lies, rather, in the simplicity of the means employed by this painter of antiquity for bodying forth his vision of the natural world.

HORSES. FROM THE HOUSE OF JULIA FELIX, POMPEII. MUSEO NAZIONALE, NAPLES.

6

SCENES OF EVERYDAY LIFE

If we leave out of account the well-defined group of pictures of a frankly classical order, inspired by Greek legends and made by neo-Attic artists, we find that the distinctive characteristic of Pompeian painting is its liveliness and popular appeal. Even in the large-scale compositions of Pompeii, Herculaneum and Stabiae it is obvious that the Campanian artist reacted against the excessive conventionality of academic, classicizing eclecticism and preferred to follow his natural bent. This instinctive urge towards a forthright, popular art supplied the vital sap that nourished the vast flowering of Campanian mural art. But for it there would be no accounting for the wonderful diversity of pictures that blossomed forth on the walls of the Pompeian houses, from the stateliest to the humblest, from sumptuous dining-rooms to modest inn parlors, from publicity posters to decorations in the family *lararia*.

Undoubtedly there existed a more or less " official " painting and we find many big decorative compositions on mythological or heroic themes. But alongside these there was a whole host of works in which the painter cast off the shackles of tradition and the neo-classical school, and set to depicting the daily life of the tradesfolk, business men, artisans and populace at large. And, making what he saw with his own eyes his starting-point, he developed new means of expression for rendering scenes and subjects that had no precedents in traditional art; in a word, he invented a new technique. To the original personalities of these artists we owe one of the most interesting aspects of Pompeian art; indeed we find a frankness and a total freedom of expression eclipsing that of any other local school of craftsmen. What is more this art throws much light on the civil and religious, public and private life of the cities of antiquity.

MARKET SCENE. FROM POMPEII. MUSEO NAZIONALE, NAPLES.

Nothing could be unfairer than categorically to decry the value of this art as far too many have thought fit to do, appraising it by the standards of Hellenistic and neo-classical art. It is *not* a minor art, nor is it a mere by-product of the great Graeco-Roman tradition. On the contrary, we do better to regard it as a spontaneous renaissance of the spirit and certain forms of the oldest pre-Roman painting: that to which we owe the superb picture of a buxom matron in the Oscan tomb at Cumae, the *Lucanian Warriors*, and the amphorae with strongly molded forms and vigorous color which figure in the *Woman Carrying an Offering* in a tomb at Paestum. The Campanian artists and artisans had the *métier* at their finger-tips and refused to be overawed by the grandiose art in favor in patrician homes; they had no qualms about rendering forms and colors as they thought fit and exhibiting their creations alongside works done in the traditional style. In fact we might draw much the same distinction between these two types of art as that which is usually drawn between provincial Roman art and the great " official " sculpture produced in Rome.

Painting of the " popular " order (like other kinds of painting) has its own scale of values. It should not be disparaged, as is too often done, because of its *laisser aller*,

LADEN MULE. FROM THE HOUSE OF JULIA FELIX, POMPEII. MUSEO NAZIONALE, NAPLES.

the sketchiness of the drawing or its seeming inability to reach the level of " high art." Even frankly popular works, in which the technique shows signs of carelessness, have an originality that is far to seek in works of the traditionalist school. Indeed it was thanks to the regenerating influence of this popular art that Campanian mural painting did not lose its vigor and lapse into a frigid, tedious reiteration of traditional compositional schemes and motifs that had lost all spiritual or cultural purport. Nor must we forget how much the early Christian art of the catacombs owed to it.

So varied was the range of subjects covered by this popular painting, as compared with other types of art, that it was, naturally enough, in great demand at all social levels. Sometimes it was of a religious order and associated with public or private acts of devotion (as in the numerous paintings found in *lararia*), or else with exotic religions, such as the cult of Isis, imported from abroad. Sometimes it illustrates the daily happenings in the Forum; or else such more spectacular occasions as the games and combats with wild beasts that took place in the great arena. Or, again, it has for its theme some such outstanding incident in the life of the city as the pitched battle between the Pompeians and the Nucerians in the Amphitheater. Nor must the fact (alluded to in previous chapters) that already in the iconographic painting we find Campanian as well as Hellenistic influences at work, be overlooked in this connection. Thus we see portraits of quite humble citizens painted with a realism very different from that of the honorific portraits in bronze or marble. Then, again, we have popular, colorful versions of ancient myths and legends, and, at the end of the scale, paintings that are frankly caricatures, products of the same *vis comica* as that which impelled the man in the street to take out his *stilus* and trace on the plaster walls of houses quaint likenesses of people who had caught his eye. In these sketches we see the typical gestures, movements and attitudes of the Campanians who thronged the markets, streets and shops of their native cities — and they were uncommonly like the crowds we see today in the older quarters of Naples.

Thus the popular painter felt under no obligation to confine himself to the well-worn themes of classical antiquity; on the contrary he put his talent to the service of the life around him, everyday reality. And, naturally enough, he found that it was by using rapid brushstrokes and small patches of color that he best could get the effect of instantaneousness and expressive vigor he was aiming at.

The procedures characteristic of this art can be seen in some pictures of horses and beasts of burden, animals far more suited for heavy work than for figuring in triumphal processions or as steeds for the immortal heroes. On a panel (one of a set of three), which falls into two parts perhaps rather arbitrarily linked together, we see on the left beside a pilaster a big mule with a pack on its back, which a man is holding by its halter. The uniform reddish-brown of its body is diversified by streaks of a lighter color, representing the harness and accentuating the spirited drawing of the legs and heads. On the other side is a group of horses and riders, to which the somewhat erratic " spotting " adds a remarkable vivacity. On another panel of the same set we see a big mule also laden with its pack; it has very long, thin, wiry legs and is jerking up its head, as if wanting to display its ornate head-stall to the best effect. Indeed so sprightly is the artist's rendering of the mule that we hardly notice the human figures near it.

In another picture, however, also a street scene, it is on the figures that our interest is focused. There are two women, one with a rather matronly air, in a tunic and dark cloak, and with her another woman so humble-looking that she seems inferior even to a servant, while facing them is a bearded old man with a bent back, leaning on a stick, who is accompanied by a dog on a lead: the typical beggar of antiquity.

Particularly interesting among works of this kind is the group of pictures called in Italy *forensi*, because they deal with Forum scenes. The big open square of the Forum at Pompeii with buildings all around provided an effective setting for the daily events of public life and the activities of the petty tradesfolk in their picturesque shops and stalls. Limited as is their scope, the *forensi* on the walls of a private house (the Villa of Julia Felix), obviously the work of the same artist, give us the most valuable illustrations we possess of everyday life at Pompeii.

They cover a great variety of subjects: market-scenes, passers-by reading the latest municipal regulations posted up between stately equestrian statues, an open-air school with the teacher and pupils watching or taking part in the punishment of a disobedient schoolboy. One of the liveliest scenes, none the less effective for being treated sketch-wise, shows us the itinerant pedlars who hawked their wares in the

OPEN-AIR MARKET IN THE FORUM. FROM THE HOUSE OF JULIA FELIX, POMPEII.

THE BAKERY. FROM POMPEII. MUSEO NAZIONALE, NAPLES.

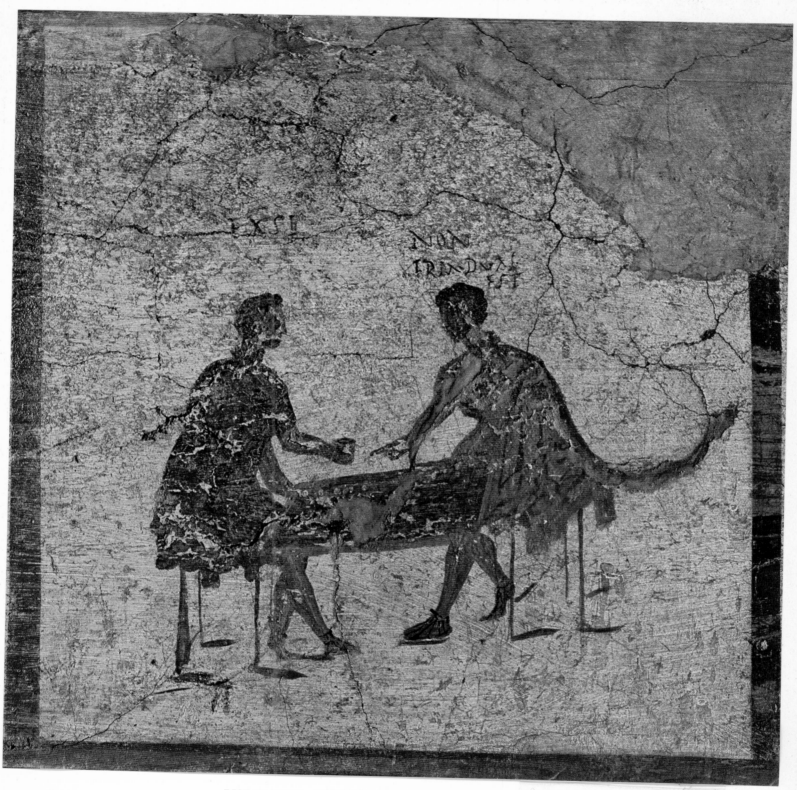

DICE-PLAYERS. FROM POMPEII. MUSEO NAZIONALE, NAPLES.

arcades of the Forum, just as they do today in the streets and squares of Naples' poorer quarters. In this well-balanced composition the figures are arranged in two groups. On the right two seated women are haggling over the price of a pair of shoes held up for their inspection by the tradesman standing in front of them, while a man looks on, waiting his turn to be served. On the left we see a vendor of crockery and household utensils, seated beside a trestle-table on which his wares are skillfully displayed; two customers, an elderly man and a youngster, are approaching, and we feel that the battle of wits between wary customer and persuasive salesman is just about to start. Though the figures and setting are little more than patches of color and contours sketchily indicated, the composition as a whole displays an admirable coherence in its distribution of space and the various groups.

Another scene, this time of a bakery, gives an entertaining glimpse of the daily life of Pompeii. Two men and a small boy, seemingly of the poorer class, are standing in front of a baker's counter on which is piled a batch of bread fresh from the oven, of just the same kind as were discovered, black and charred, in the ovens of Pompeii and Herculaneum. On the salesman's right is a basket containing cakes, and more loaves are stacked behind him in a sort of bin. The two slow-gestured, stolid-looking customers wear dark purple tunics; one of them has slung over his tunic an orange-yellow cape which is bathed in the full light of the morning sun. The boy, his arms outstretched, seems pathetically eager to be given the loaf that is being handed across the counter by the baker, who, perched on his high stool, looks down on the little group with the lordly air of a judge seated on his bench. The attitudes of the various figures suggest that we have here a *congiarium*, *i.e.* a free distribution of bread to the poor.

We get an even better insight into the everyday life of the Pompeian populace in the tavern *(caupona)* scenes, with their motley crowd of *habitués* and casuals, loving couples and solitary topers, loafers and rowdies, pedlars and pimps, on all of whom the inn-keeper keeps a watchful eye. Some of his customers are in a hurry and only stop for a " quick one " at the bar-counter giving on the street, while others, who have settled down for a leisurely meal in the back parlor, are having a game of dice to see who will stand the drinks. It is interesting to observe that the walls of these taverns were adorned with genre scenes of all descriptions, just as were the walls of Italian 19th-century cafés. These little pictures, combining entertainment with publicity in quite the modern manner, have inscriptions inviting the guests to enjoy themselves, but at the same time to behave with due propriety. Imbued as it was with a homely realism smacking of the soil, this art was perfectly suited to the customers' tastes and their condition of life. Against the neutral or faintly tinted background of the wall, the figures stand out vigorously; stiff, puppet-like gestures accentuate their jerky movements and facial expressions. Faces are painted in subdued, opaque hues, while the clothes have the gaudy colors typical of plebeian taste. The liveliest scene of all is one of men engaged in a dice game, some calmly seated, others wrangling, while the varying chances of the game are reflected in the gestures and faces of the onlookers. A young waiter is serving drinks to the players; his attitude of mingled

THE POMPEIAN VENUS. SHOP-SIGN FROM THE PREMISES OF VERECUNDUS, POMPEII.

contempt and deference is that of a worldly-wise youngster who has nothing left to learn about the vices of his elders.

We find similar methods employed in the pictures made for purposes of publicity and commissioned by enterprising merchants and business men for adorning the façades of their premises. Sometimes religious motifs were combined with the purely commercial elements. A striking example is the front wall of the establishment of a man named Verecundus, a cloth-maker *(vestiarius)* who kept shop in the " Street of Abundance," the area of the new excavations. The entire façade is elaborately decorated: above is Venus Pompeiana, the tutelary goddess of the city, and, below, a shop-sign, showing the workshop with the employees dressing the cloth. It is interesting to note the very different manners in which this popular painter handled his two subjects, iconographic and commercial. He paints Venus in a spirit of humble piety and spares no pains in producing an image worthy of the goddess, using a rich, colorful palette, and obviously determined to give of his best. In the advertisement picture, on the other hand, his technique verges on the slapdash, drawing is confined to essentials, and the work is hardly more than a monochrome sketch.

His conception of Venus, moreover, was quite a new one. We are not shown a laughter-loving Aphrodite or an amorous young goddess hastening to a rendezvous with Mars; on the contrary, standing proudly erect in a chariot drawn by elephants, with her turreted crown and scepter, the Pompeian Venus cuts an hieratic, majestic, almost Oriental figure. Cupid is at her side, two winged Erotes hover in the air beside her, and in the foreground, right and left, stand two Lares (tutelary deities). The four elephants are painted head on, as if bearing down on the spectator, with their lumbering bodies fanning out on either side, and their trunks converging on the center of the foreground. The general lay-out of this picture is curiously reminiscent of an altarpiece with the Madonna and attendant saints and angels; while the prosaic scene below might well be one of those predellas in which the Italian artists depicted incidents in the life of the pious donor commissioning the altarpiece. Indeed, with this painting and some others equally " advanced " in theme and spirit, we are on the very threshold of the Christian art of the catacombs; a new age was dawning and the great cycle of Pompeian painting, so miraculously to be preserved for future generations, had run its destined course.

BIBLIOGRAPHY

GENERAL

WICKHOFF, F. *Roman Art*, London 1900 (trans. by Mrs. S. A. STRONG).

HERRMANN, P. - BRUCKMANN, F. *Denkmäler der Malerei des Altertums*, Munich 1904 etc.

REINACH, A. *Recueil Milliet, Textes grecs et latins relatifs à l'histoire de la peinture ancienne*, Paris 1921.

REINACH, S. *Répertoire des peintures grecques et romaines*, Paris 1922.

PFUHL, E. *Meisterwerke griechischer Zeichnung und Malerei*, Munich 1924.

PFUHL, E. *Masterpieces of Greek Drawing and Painting*, London 1926.

Monumenti della pittura antica scoperti in Italia, Libreria dello Stato, Rome 1935 etc.

BIBLIOGRAPHY BY CHAPTER-HEADINGS

1. PRE-ROMAN PAINTING :

WEEGE, F. *Oskische Grabmalerei*, " Jahrbuch des Deutschen Archaeologischen Instituts," XXIV, 1909, p. 99 ff.

2. OFFICIAL PAINTING IN ROME :

RIZZO, G. E. *Le pitture della Casa dei Grifi (Palatino) ; Le pitture della Casa di Livia (Palatino) ; Le pitture dell'Aula Isiaca di Caligola (Palatino) ;* in " Monumenti della Pittura Antica scoperti in Italia," Sec. III, fasc. I, II and III, Rome.

3. THE FARNESINA HOUSE :

MAU, A. " Annali dell'Istituto di Corrispondenza archeologica," 1882, p. 301, and " Monumenti dell'Istituto," XII, plates 5-8, 17-34.

LESSING, J. - MAU, A. *Wand- und Deckenschmuck eines römischen Hauses aus der Zeit des Augustus*, Berlin 1891.

LOEWY, E. *Aneddoti giudiziari dipinti su un fregio antico*, " Rendiconti Accademia dei Lincei," 1897, p. 27.

4. THE ALDOBRANDINI WEDDING AND THE ODYSSEY LANDSCAPES :

NOGARA, B. *Le Nozze Aldobrandini e Paesaggi con scene dell'Odissea e le altre pitture murali antiche conservate nella Biblioteca Vaticana e nei Musei Pontifici*, U. Hoepli, Milan 1917.

5. POMPEII AND CAMPANIA :

Standard Works :

MAU, A. *Pompeii, its Life and Art* (translated by F. W. Kelsey), New York, London 1899 ; *Pompeji in Leben und Kunst*, Leipzig 1900.

CARRINGTON, R. C. *Pompeii* (in English and French), 1936.

MAIURI, A. *Pompeii*, Collection *Visioni Italiche*, Novara (published in English, French, German and Italian) 1938, 1943, 1952 ; *Pompeii, Herculaneum (Itinerari dei Musei e Monumenti d'Italia)*, Libreria dello Stato, Rome (published in English, French, German, Italian and Spanish) 1949-1951.

Catalogues :

HELBIG, W. *Wandgemälde der vom Vesuv verschütteten Städte Campaniens*, Leipzig 1868.

SOGLIANO, A. *Le pitture murali campane scoperte negli anni 1867-79* (supplement to Helbig's work), Naples 1879.

RUESCH, A. *Guida del Museo Nazionale di Napoli*, mosaics pp. 53-62, paintings pp. 288-350 (in the old grouping), 1911.

ELIA, O. *Pitture murali e mosaici nel Museo Nazionale di Napoli*, Rome, Libreria dello Stato, 1932 (partly in the old grouping).

Special Works :

MAU, A. *Geschichte der dekorativen Wandmalerei in Pompeji*, Berlin, Reiner 1882.

CURTIUS, L. *Die Wandmalerei Pompejis*, Leipzig 1929.

RIZZO, G. E. *La pittura ellenistico-romana*, Treves, Milan 1929.

MARCONI, P. *La pittura dei Romani*, Rome 1929.

SWINDLER, M. H. *Ancient Painting*, New Haven 1929.

SCHEFOLD, K. *Pompejanische Malerei, Sinn und Ideengeschichte*, Basel 1952.

Monographs and Studies :

HELBIG, W. *Untersuchungen über die campanische Wandmalerei*, Leipzig 1873.

RODENWALDT, G. *Die Komposition der pompeianischen Wandgemälde*, Berlin 1909.

DIEPOLDER, H. *Untersuchungen zur Komposition der römisch-campanischen Wandgemälde*, " Römische Mitteilungen," XLI, 1926, p. 1 ff.

WIRTH, F. *Der Stil der kampanischen Wandgemälde im Verhältnis zur Wanddekoration*, " Römische Mitteilungen," LII, 1927, p. 1 ff.

BEYEN, H. G. *Die pompejanische Wanddekoration vom zweiten bis zum vierten Stil*, The Hague 1938.

BIANCHI BANDINELLI, R. *Tradizione ellenistica e gusto romano nella pittura pompeiana*, " Critica d'arte," I and II, 1941.

ELIA, O. *Note per uno studio della decorazione parietale a Pompei*, " Pompeiana, Studi per il 2º centenario degli scavi," Naples 1952.

WIRTH, *Römische Wandmalerei vom Untergang Pompejis bis Hadrian*, " Römische Mitteilungen," XLIV, p. 91 ff.

Technical Procedures :

DONNER, O. *Die erhaltenen antiken Wandmalereien in technischer Beziehung*, in HELBIG, W. *Wandgemälde der vom Vesuv verschütteten Städte Campaniens*, pp. I-CXXVII, 1868.

LAURIE, A. P. *Greek and Roman Methods of Painting*, London 1910.

EIBNER, A. *Wandmalerei*, Munich 1926.

VAN BUREN, A. W. *Further Pompeian Studies*, " Memoirs of the American Academy in Rome," X, 1932, pp. 40-53 (on the alteration of the original colors).

DEUBNER, O. *Expolitio, Inkrustation und Wandmalerei*, " Römische Mitteilungen," LIV, 1939, pp. 14-41.

MAIURI, A. *Picturae lignei formis inclusae - Note sulla tecnica della pittura campana*, " Rendiconti Accademia d'Italia," series VII, vol. I, 1940, p. 138 ff.

SELIM AUGUSTI. *La tecnica dell'antica pittura parietale pompeiana*, "Pompeiana, Studi per il 2º centenario degli scavi di Pompei," Naples 1950, pp. 313-354.

6. VILLA OF THE MYSTERIES :

RIZZO, G. E. *Dionysos mystes*, "Memorie dell'Accademia di Archeologia, Lettere e Belle Arti di Napoli," vol. III, 1914, p. 93 ff.

BIEBER, M. *Der Mysteriensaal der Villa Item*, "Jahrbuch des Deutschen Archaeologischen Instituts," XLIII, 1928, p. 323 ff.

MAIURI, A. *La Villa dei Misteri*, Libreria dello Stato, Rome, 1930. (2nd ed. 1947 : 2 vols. with 18 color plates.)

MARCONI, P. *Il fregio dionisiaco della Villa dei Misteri*, Bergamo 1938.

BIANCHI BANDINELLI, R. *Noterella in margine ai problemi della pittura antica*, "Storicità dell'arte," 1943, p. 165 ff.

MAIURI, A. *Note e commenti al dipinto della Villa dei Misteri*, "La Parola del Passato," fasc. VIII, 1948, p. 185 ff.

7. VILLA BOSCOREALE :

STUDNICZKA, F. *Imagines illustrium - Frühhellenische Bildnisgruppen in den Wandbildern des Hauptsaals von Boscoreale*, "Jahrbuch des Deutschen Archaeologischen Instituts," 1923, p. 64 ff.

BARNABEI, F. *La villa pompeiana di P. Fannio Sinistore*, Rome 1901.

SAMBON, *Les fresques de Boscoreale*, Paris-Naples n.d.

8. BASILICA OF HERCULANEUM :

GABRIEL, MABEL M. *Masters of Campanian Painting*, New York, 1952 pp. 7-34.

9. THE ALEXANDER MOSAIC :

PERNICE, E. *Bemerkungen zum Alexandermosaik*, "Römische Mitteilungen," XXII, 1907, p. 25 ; XXIII, 1908, p. 11.

WINTER, FR. *Das Alexandermosaik aus Pompeji*, Strasbourg 1909.

PFUHL, E. *Malerei und Zeichnung*, p. 757 ff.

FUHRMANN, A. *Philoxenos vom Eretria*, Göttingen 1931.

10. EPIC THEMES — GODS, HEROES, MYTHS AND SACRED RITES:

RIZZO, G. E. *Le pitture della Casa del Poeta tragico*, "Monumenti della Pittura antica," sec. III, 1935.

ELIA, O. *Le pitture della Casa del Citarista*, "Monumenti della Pittura antica," sec. III, Pompeii, fasc. I, 1937.

MAIURI, A. *Le pitture della Casa di M. Fabius Amandio, del Sacerdos Amandus e di P. Cornelius Teges*, "Monumenti della Pittura antica," sec. III, Pompeii, fasc. II, 1938.

ELIA, O. *Le pitture del Tempio d'Iside*, "Monumenti della Pittura antica," sec. III, Fasc. III, 1941.

GABRIEL, MABEL M. *Masters of Campanian Painting*, New York 1952, pp. 35-50.

11. THE THEATER :

BIEBER, M. - RODENWALDT, G. *Die Mosaiken des Dioscurides von Samos*, "Jahrbuch des Deutschen Archaeologischen Instituts," XXXVI, 1911, pp. 1-22.

MAIURI, A. *Il ritratto del Menandro nella Casa delle argenterie a Pompei*, "Bollettino d'Arte," December 1931 ; cf. *La Casa del Menandro*, p. 106 ff.

PERNICE, E. *Pavimente und figürliche Mosaiken*, Berlin 1938, p. 169 ff.

BIEBER, M. *The History of the Greek and Roman Theater*, (2nd ed.) Princeton 1939.

12. THE PORTRAIT :

GUSMAN, P. *Les portraits à Pompéi*, "Revue de l'art ancien et moderne," X, 1897, pp. 343-350.

DE FRANCISCIS, A. *Il ritratto romano a Pompei*, "Memorie dell'Accademia di Archeologia, Lettere e Belle Arti di Napoli," I, 1951 (limited to portraits in bronze and marble).

13. THE GENRE SCENE :

ROBERT, "Winckelmannsprogramm," XXI 1897, XXII 1898, XXIII 1899 ; "Hermes," XXXVI, 1901, p. 368 ff. (on the Herculaneum monochromes).

MAIURI, A., *La parodia di Enea*, "Bollettino d'Arte," 1950, p. 198 ff.

BRENDEL, O. *Allegorie des pompejanischen Totenkopf-Mosaiks*, "Römische Mitteilungen," XLIX, 1934, p. 157 ff.

14. LANDSCAPE :

ROSTOVTZEV, M. *Hellenistisch-römische Architekturlandschaft*, "Römische Mitteilungen," 1911, p. 48 ff.

GRIMAL, P. *Les Métamorphoses d'Ovide et la peinture paysagiste de l'époque d'Auguste*, "Revue d'Etudes latines," XVI, fasc. I, 1938, p. 145 ff. ; *Les jardins romains à la fin de la République et aux deux premiers siècles de l'Empire*, "Bibliothèque des Ecoles françaises d'Athènes et de Rome," CLV, 1943, Boccard, Paris.

DAWSON, M. C. *Romano-campanian Mythological Landscape Painting*, "Yale Classical Studies," IX, New Haven 1944.

MAIURI, A. *Nuove pitture di giardino a Pompei*, "Bollettino d'Arte," I, (January-March) 1952.

15. THE STILL LIFE :

BEYEN, H. G. *Ueber Stilleben aus Pompeji und Herculaneum*, The Hague 1928.

RIZZO, G. E. *Le pitture di natura morta* (fascicule not yet published in "Monumenti della pittura antica scoperti in Italia "), Libreria dello Stato, Rome, 1935.

CASELLA, D. *La frutta nella pittura pompeiana*, "Pompeiana, Studi per il 2º centenario degli scavi di Pompei," 1950.

PALOMBI, A. *La fauna marina nei mosaici e nei dipinti*, "Pompeiana, Studi per il 2º centenario degli scavi di Pompei," 1950, pp. 425-455.

16. EVERYDAY LIFE :

TANZER, H. H. *The Common People of Pompeii*, "The Johns Hopkins University Studies in Archeology," Nº 29, Baltimore 1939.

INDEX OF NAMES AND SUBJECTS

THE COLORPLATES

The list of colorplates follows the alphabetical order of the places in which the originals were found

CONTENTS

THIS VOLUME OF THE COLLECTION

THE GREAT CENTURIES OF PAINTING

WAS PRINTED

BOTH TEXT AND COLORPLATES

BY THE

SKIRA

COLOR STUDIO

AT IMPRIMERIES RÉUNIES S. A.

LAUSANNE

FINISHED THE TENTH DAY OF MARCH

NINETEEN HUNDRED AND FIFTY-THREE

*All the work produced by the Skira Color Studio
is carried out by the technical staff of
Editions d'Art Albert Skira*

PRINTED IN SWITZERLAND